Mastering
Presentations

Mastering
Presentations

Be the **Undisputed Expert**
When You Deliver Presentations
(Even if You Feel Like You're
Going to **Throw Up**)

DOUG STANEART

WILEY

John Wiley & Sons, Inc.

Cover image: Seminar @ Joshua Hodge Photography/istockphoto
Cover design: John Wiley & Sons, Inc.

Published by John Wiley & Sons, Inc., Hoboken, New Jersey.
Published simultaneously in Canada.

For general information about our other products and services, please contact our Customer Care Department within the United States at (800) 762-2974, outside the United States at (317) 572-3993 or fax (317) 572-4002.

Wiley publishes in a variety of print and electronic formats and by print-on-demand. Some material included with standard print versions of this book may not be included in e-books or in print-on-demand. If this book refers to media such as a CD or DVD that is not included in the version you purchased, you may download this material at http://booksupport.wiley.com. For more information about Wiley products, visit www.wiley.com.

Library of Congress Cataloging-in-Publication Data:

Staneart, Doug, 1971–
    Mastering presentations : be the undisputed expert when you deliver presentations (even if you feel like you're going to throw up) / Doug Staneart.
       p. cm.
    Includes index.
    ISBN 978-1-118-48430-2 (pbk.); ISBN 978-1-118-49416-5 (ebk);
    ISBN 978-1-118-49426-4 (ebk); ISBN 978-1-118-49428-8 (ebk)
       1. Business presentations.   2. Public speaking.   I. Title.
    HF5718.22.S738   2013
    658.4'52—dc23
                                                                            2012030205

Printed in the United States of America
10 9 8 7 6 5 4 3 2 1

To the more than 12,000 Fearless Presentation graduates who were my "lab class" for the concepts in this book. Thanks, everyone!

Contents

CONTENTS

Introduction: Why This Book Was Written

"Just about everything that you have ever learned about public speaking is wrong!"

—Doug Staneart

When I gave my first business presentation, I was absolutely terrified.

I was just a few months away from graduating from college, and I was an intern for a huge oil company at a time when the price of oil had plummeted to about $16 per barrel. We were told that in earlier years that as long as an intern did a good job while working for the company, the company almost always extended an invitation for a full-time position upon graduation. However, I was in the acquisitions and divestitures (A&D) department of the company during the internship, and for the entire time that I was there, we never acquired any oil properties or oil interests. We were selling everything. As we did, more of the full-time employees were being laid off and being hired back as temporary contract workers.

I could see the handwriting on the wall, so I called the director who was in charge of the intern program and asked her what the real prospects were of me actually having a job when I graduated. She paused for a good 4 or 5 seconds before answering the question. She said, "Doug, my understanding is that, in this economy, we are probably only likely to permanently hire, at most, 4 of the 20 interns. In fact, I just found out that the company is discontinuing the intern program for at least one year."

"Are you out of a job?" I asked her.

"No, it is not quite that bad yet. The company is moving me to Bakersfield. It is a lateral move, but they are taking care of me. By the way, you've got a good shot at getting one of the permanent positions, because of your experience in A&D. Just do well in your exit presentation, because some of the vice presidents have been impressed with your work so far." I knew what she really meant, though; I had a good shot at getting hired because I'd work for a salary that was about a third the size of the employees who were getting laid off.

At that point in my life, I had been told that to be successful, I had to go to school, get a good job, work my way up the corporate ladder, and become chief executive officer (CEO) by the time I was 34. Now what I saw was my entire future at stake, and this particular future depended almost entirely on a single 15-minute presentation. No pressure, right?

In school, I had always been a decent speaker. My presentations were nothing to write home about, but I muddled through them as I advanced from one grade to the next. I had also been an elected officer in a couple of clubs, so I didn't feel like I needed a lot of help presenting. However, the semester before I started the internship, I took a class called Business Communications. My entire grade that semester was determined by three presentations that I delivered about three or four weeks apart. On the first presentation, the graduate student who was teaching the class gave me a 94 percent which was an A. Immediately after the presentation, she gave me a pretty fair critique. She complimented me on my content and delivery, but she gave me a couple of items to work on before the next presentation. She told me that I said *uhm* seven times in the presentation and that it was a distraction. She also told me that when I stuck my right hand into my pocket, I looked nervous.

I spent the next three weeks working on saying *uhm* less and keeping my hand out of my pocket when I practiced. I said *uhm* 14 times during the second presentation, and I ended up getting an 84 percent. I didn't stick my hand in my pocket, but every time I caught myself almost sticking my hand in my pocket, I would stop abruptly, and I reacted in an odd way. I also knew that the teacher was counting off how often I said *uhm,* and it threw me.

When I delivered my third presentation, I focused very little time on the content and spent a lot of time on trying to fix what my teacher was telling me were problems. I ended up getting a 74 percent on the third presentation. I ended up with a B in the class, but I was just glad there wasn't a fourth presentation. When the class was over, for the first time in my life, I felt like a failure as a presenter. I got worse every time that I presented, so I assumed something was wrong with me.

About four months later, I was at the top of a skyscraper in downtown Dallas giving a presentation to all of my peers (the other interns who were competing against me for these four permanent positions), the head of the intern program, my boss, all of the other interns' bosses, and three vice presidents from the home office.

When I walked into the room, I was the only person who wasn't wearing a jacket. (I didn't even own a jacket.) My nervousness edged up even more.

The first presenter was introduced, and he stood up and started with a joke. When everyone was laughing, I could tell that the speaker relaxed. His presentation was lively and somewhat entertaining. (I didn't have any jokes . . .)

Second up was the woman who worked with me in A&D, and she gave a great presentation about a single project that she and I had worked on that summer. She had the marketing department create some colored slides for her overhead projector. (I didn't have any visual aids . . .) I had assumed that the presentation had to be about what I did the entire summer, so my presentation wasn't very focused. I hadn't even thought about picking just one of the cool things that I had accomplished and delivering the entire presentation on just that one thing.

I was panicking. I was next, and I knew that what I had designed and prepared wasn't even close to the level of the first two presentations. I could feel the beads of sweat forming on my palms and also on my forehead. My heart was racing as I walked to the front. Since I didn't have any visual aids, I turned back to the flip chart behind me and tried to draw Oklahoma (where I had spent a lot of time working); it ended up looking like a lame parallelogram. I started speaking, and I spoke really, really quickly. I gave my 15-minute presentation in a little over 5 minutes; I said every single word, so I knew I was zooming through my presentation.

I rushed back to my seat, and I was hoping that a black hole would open up under the table and suck me in. I didn't want to have to face any of the people in that room. I didn't want to have to look them in the eye. I was so embarrassed that I wanted to flee the room. But I had to stay there and listen to presenter after presenter—all of whom did a much better job than I did. I was devastated. I knew that I had just destroyed any hope that I had of getting my dream job.

I got mad. I got so mad that I told myself that I would never fail like that again. Over the next year, I began to study great presenters. My dad had invited me to a business conference where a number of professional speakers were presenting. One of them was Bob Burg, who stood up on stage without any notes or visual aids and had the crowd in the palm of his hand. Bob was promoting his new book at the time, called *Endless Referrals,* and because I loved his speech so much, I bought the book at the conference. I read the book in a couple of weeks and was hooked. Every nonfiction book that I had ever read before this one I had found to be boring and not very helpful. But this one was practical. In the next few months, I read a couple of more books that I had checked out at the library. I read each one of them even faster than the first.

I began to see that my success had little to do with how many degrees I had acquired or how much money I had. I realized that if I wanted to succeed, I just had to make the decision to do so.

About that same time, I had been nominated by one of my professors to be the international student of the year for my degree. This was based on my grades, the organizations to which I belonged, and the work that I had done in the industry prior to graduation. But after a few months, since I hadn't heard anything, I assumed that I didn't win the award.

I graduated from college and was lucky enough to get a job earning about $20,000 per year (which was just under the poverty level in my area). But I knew that this first job was a stepping-stone. A month or so after starting this job, the association that regulated my industry called to say that the officers had chosen me to receive the student of the year award. They wanted to fly me in to the international convention to accept the award.

I knew that I'd have to give a short presentation when I accepted the award, but I wasn't the least bit scared this time. In fact, during the evening of the presentation, as I was walking through the crowd, I met the woman who had previously been in charge of the intern program. She seemed genuinely happy to see me again. During our conversation, she mentioned that the layoffs at her company had continued and that she was one of the latest casualties. There were more than 300 people in our location who worked on contracts when I was at the company; a year later, they had downsized to only three permanent people working on these same oil contracts.

I was feeling kind of smug now, because I began to see that the failure I had experienced just a year before had been a blessing in disguise. She asked me if the company that I was working for had sent me to the conference, and I told her that the association had invited me and paid my way. When I told her about the award, I smiled inside when she looked at me and said, "You?!" I could tell that she was confused, because the last impression that she had of me was the bumbling stumbling kid who blew the big speech. What a difference a year makes!

Later that evening, just before I was announced as the award winner, I was thinking, "What would Bob do?" referring to Bob Burg, who I had seen captivate the crowd less than a year prior. When I delivered my acceptance speech, I started with a funny, self-deprecating story based on my short time in the oil business. Just as the first guy who presented in the boardroom the year before, the laughter from the crowd made me feel more relaxed. When I finished, I received a huge round of applause and had dozens of people come up to me afterward to compliment me on my speech.

Within six months from the time that I delivered that presentation, I had received almost a dozen job offers from people who were in the audience (the price of oil has risen sharply). I turned them all down, though. I had realized that if I spent the next 30 years working for a big company, then my potential success would always be determined by someone else. I knew that I was capable of more.

I spent the next eight years studying with some of the most successful salespeople and presenters in the world, and in 2002, I founded The Leader's Institute. Since then, I have personally trained more than 20,000 presenters, as well as some of the most successful presentation coaches in the world. I didn't have all of the answers when I started, but over the past decade, our team has uncovered some little known *presentation secrets* and worked extremely hard to make presentations easy.

Since I wrote my first book, *Fearless Presentations,* in 2002, I have traveled all over the world to teach presentation skills. In fact, just in the past year or so, I have delivered professional speeches on the island of Madeira, Portugal; in Frankfurt, Germany; in Dublin and London; and in every major city in the United States, from Anchorage to Miami and from New England to San Diego. I've had the privilege of visiting 47 states and more than 15 different countries. And I've been able to accomplish all of these things primarily because I present well. Every time I speak, I generate, on average, about $10,000 per speech. (Trust me, if the kid who blew the intern speech can become a professional speaker and the expert in his field, you can too!)

Since I founded The Leader's Institute, my instructors and I have been able to uncover some pretty important presentation secrets that I will be sharing with you in this book. Follow our simple guidelines, and you will become the expert in your field.

CHAPTER 1

The Presenter Who Speaks with Poise and Confidence Is Always Seen as the Expert

"What makes a king out of a slave? Courage!"
—The Cowardly Lion, *The Wizard of Oz*

After the German surrender in World War I, the Treaty of Versailles was signed, giving a number of German territories to surrounding countries. When Hitler came to power, one of his main goals was to reunite the lost cities with the "fatherland." By August 1939, he had succeeded in reacquiring each of the lost German cities, except for one. The Treaty of Versailles gave the city of Danzig to Poland, which gave the Polish people a land route to the Baltic Sea, referred to as the Polish Corridor. The corridor made this tiny city vitally important to the Polish economy. But this last city was also symbolic to the German people, because with Danzig added back into Germany, the Treaty of Versailles was entirely void. So when Hitler requested access to this corridor and Poland refused, war between Poland and Germany was imminent.

In September, Poland turned to Great Britain for help and the two countries signed an Agreement of Mutual Assistance. This assured Poland that if Germany tried to take Danzig, Great Britain and her ally France would likely go to war with Germany. Although the agreement with England gave Hitler pause, the goal to reunite the fallen Germany was too tempting, and Germany and their new ally, the Soviet Union, invaded.

As the new head of state for England, King George VI was responsible for announcing that Great Britain would again be going to war with Germany, but King George had a big problem. King George suffered from a chronic stammer, making simple words almost impossible for him to pronounce. He had particular trouble with the letter *k* (which had the potential for great embarrassment for a *k*ing). Prior to the speech, he had spent years working with a speech therapist, Lionel Logue, who helped him reduce this stammer, but King George was on the verge of the biggest, most important speech of his life. The pressure was mounting.

On September 3, 1939, King George VI had to address his subjects to inform them that "for the second time in the lives of most of us, we are at war." For a little less than 6 minutes, the king spoke without stuttering or stammering. His poise and confidence were an inspiration to the British people. For literally the first time in his young reign, England saw King George as a real leader and a powerful statesman.

The British people needed a calming voice to relieve their fear of the imminent war "that would not be on the battlefield, but on their doorsteps." What would have happened if King George had addressed the people with the hesitation and the nervousness that had plagued him for most of his life? This one successful presentation changed King George and changed the future of Europe.

The Person Who Speaks with Confidence Is Always Seen as the Expert

People judge our competence by the confidence that we show when we stand up and speak, and the person who can stand up and say what he or she wants to say with poise will always be seen as an expert in his or her field. Conversely, the person who can't speak confidently will have a hard time convincing others that he or she is a leader.

Let's say, God forbid, that you get appendicitis, and you have to have your appendix removed. Prior to the operation, the surgeon enters your room and describes the procedure to you. However, just before he speaks, you see a quiver in his lip and notice his hands trembling slightly. As he begins to tell you about the operation, he speaks in choppy sentences and even loses his place for a moment and seems confused.

There is a good chance that no matter how much pain you are in, you will be clamoring to get a second opinion immediately. This surgeon may have graduated at the top of his class and may have even written a number of books on the subject, but that initial perception that he is generating is one of insecurity and incompetence. It would be even worse if he rolled in the PowerPoint slide show so that he wouldn't forget anything.

The point is that the confidence that a person shows when standing up to speak is often perceived by others to be competence in what he or she does. Stand and speak with poise and confidence about a subject that you know thoroughly, and your audience will always see you as being the expert in that field. In fact, if all other things are equal between two people, the one who speaks well will always be seen as more competent than the one who speaks poorly (or not at all).

Early in my career, I volunteered to speak at local business events in my hometown, and I began to build for myself a reputation of being a pretty good speaker. One of the vice presidents of a national financial planning firm saw me speak at a couple of events, and he pulled me aside after one of my presentations to discuss a problem that he was having. He told me that his company used local seminars as a way to attract potential new clients to their firm, and he had been looking for a person to lead their seminars.

"All my guys are thoroughly trained in securities, trading, financial planning, and even insurance, but when we invite potential customers to our meetings, we need someone who can really build that trust with the people in the audience," he explained. "We are one of the, if not *the,* most successful financial planning companies in the world, but we really need someone who can portray that to an audience." His idea was to hire me on a contract basis and have me "wow" the audience and build a rapport with them. Then we would let his financial planners follow up with the investors after the presentation.

I understood his thought process, but his plan would have a tough time succeeding. One of the main benefits of being a good presenter is that your words carry a lot of weight with the audience, and if you do a great job, you can really build trust and rapport with them. So if I, someone outside of his company, were his speaker, his audiences might like and even trust me, but when I left the room, that trust would evaporate—especially if immediately after I left, the folks who were having trouble speaking to groups in the first place took over. The trade-off would have been awkward and clumsy.

What I suggested to him instead was to train his financial planners to present more confidently. Public speaking is just like any other skill and can be learned. In fact, it can be learned very quickly and easily if you use a step-by-step process. Once that confidence is gained, the presenters have a strategic advantage in the marketplace. It took us about six months, but by the end of the process, each of his financial planners were leading their own seminars and building their client list significantly month after month. The words that they spoke in their seminars and the way that they carried themselves portrayed their expertise in their industry. Keep in mind that they were always the experts, but before they improved their presentations, the audiences who they spoke to just didn't see it.

This company's situation was like having a Lamborghini and keeping it in the garage under a protective cover. They knew what they had, but the world never got to see it. If you have one of the fastest and coolest cars on the planet, then you have to drive it. Once they started "driving," their revenue and client base increased exponentially.

If you have an expertise that the business world or consumers need, then you have to let the world know about it. Public speaking is one of the fastest and easiest ways to let the world know that you are an expert. (Incidentally, it is often a form of free publicity. Or in some of cases, people will actually pay you to do it. Literally— customers will actually pay you to market to them!)

Look for places where your prospective customers gather and volunteer to share your expertise with them. For instance, if you are an insurance agent, offer to speak at the local multiple listing service (MLS) meeting or Realtor Association meeting, because if someone buys a new house, they will also need insurance for it. You could let these realtors know about trends in insurance rates that might cause a sale to stall or how to help their clients combine policies to save and lower their monthly escrow payments, which lowers the amount due each month for their mortgage.

Or if you are a banker, you might volunteer to speak at a local small-business association meeting or small-business breakfast and teach the attendees how to write a business plan that is likely to help them get a small-business loan. Or a banker might speak at colleges or universities to help young people avoid falling into the trap of incurring too much debt. This same banker might even partner with a financial planner and do a seminar for clients on how to lower their mortgage payments so that they can invest more in their retirement.

YOU ARE THE EXPERT

Regardless of what industry you are in or what expertise you have, you first have to realize that you are the expert at something and the knowledge that you have is valuable to someone. When I was 14 years old, my dad owned a home remodeling company, and every winter, I crawled under houses to help him repair frozen pipes that had burst. After a couple of winters, I had so much experience doing this, that I could do it in my sleep. By the time I was a teenager, I was an expert at repairing ruptured PVC pipes. After I graduated college, my first real job was working for an oil company doing title work for mineral rights. After a couple of years, not only had I gotten pretty good at it, but I had also trained a number of new people. My third year in the training industry, I generated a half-million dollars' worth of sales for the first time, and that same year, I also received a couple of awards for outstanding instruction. It took me five years as an entrepreneur to attain my first million dollars, but it took only about eight more months to generate my second million. With each of these accomplishments, I became the expert, because I had information that the general public didn't have (even when my expertise was repairing frozen pipes).

Don't underestimate your knowledge. Your experience has made you the expert.

One of my friends in college was going to school to be an elementary schoolteacher, and she absolutely hated math. However, once she graduated, she found out that in the state of Texas, math and science teachers were in high demand and were therefore paid an extra fee. Knowing this, she decided to become a fourth grade math teacher. Those of us who knew her pretty well were laughing when we asked her about her career choice, because for the three or four years that we had known her, she complained repeatedly about the basic math, algebra, and trigonometry classes that she had to take in school. These classes were her nemeses. After a little teasing from us, she replied by saying, "In order to teach fourth grade math, I just have to be an expert at fifth grade math," and I learned a prophetic life lesson. To be an expert at something, you just need to have a little more knowledge than your audience.

For instance, let's say that you are a restaurant manager who turned around a struggling location. How many other managers in the world would want to hear how you did it? You'd be the expert at restaurant turnarounds (especially if you were able to do it a second or third time). Or say you are a dentist who excels at getting your patients to show up for every six-month checkup. Other dentists would pay dearly to figure out how you do it. Whatever you do on a day-to-day basis makes you the expert at that activity.

Because you are the expert, you have credibility in the marketplace.

After teaching presentation skills classes for about 10 years, I received a contract to teach presentation skills and leadership for members of the Associated General Contractors of America. After teaching classes for these member companies for a couple of years, the participants began to think of me as being an expert in the commercial construction industry. Keep in mind that I had never once built a big skyscraper. In fact, I knew very little about the day-to-day operations of general contractors. However, because I had worked with so many general contractors in that first couple of years, I had more expertise in the industry than other leadership and presentation coaches. I had developed a specialty.

A friend of mine did the same. He decided that every sales trainer targets car dealerships as potential customers, so instead, he decided to specialize in conducting sales training for salespeople who sell trailer houses. He had very little competition in this industry and quickly became the go-to expert.

One of my clients hired me to coach a few of his employees who were preparing for what he called a short list presentation, which was a presentation where a short list of qualified vendors were competing for a very large contract. Although everyone in the room knew more about building skyscrapers than I did, I knew way more about designing and delivering presentations than any of them did. With my coaching, they were able to borrow my expertise to deliver their presentation in a much more fluid and effective way.

After doing this kind of training a few times with some pretty remarkable success, I quickly became known as the short list presentation coach, and I had developed a brand-new expertise.

Ask yourself, "What am I really, really good at?" and you will quickly find out what your expertise is. Once you realize that you are the expert, the rest is relatively easy.

CHAPTER 2

A Simple Way to Design Presentations in 15 Minutes or Less

"If you want me to give you a two-hour presentation, I am ready today. If you want only a five-minute speech, it will take me two weeks to prepare."
—Mark Twain

Okay, so now that we realize how much of an expert you really are, how do we start designing compelling speeches or presentations that people in your industry really want to listen to? More important, how do we design this compelling presentation without it taking hours, days, or even weeks? The first step is to realize that what the audience really wants to know and what you really want to tell them are often two *totally* different things.

What the Audience Wants to Know and What You Want to Tell Them Are Often Two Totally Different Things

Perhaps the biggest mistakes that people make when they start to design a presentation is to ask themselves, "Okay, so what do I know about this subject?" They then start designing slides based on everything that they know. What happens more often than not is that they end up with too much information and too many slides, so to fit the time frame allotted, they will cut some content. When this happens, what presenters end up with is a Swiss cheese presentation that is both difficult to remember (to deliver) and difficult for the audience to retain.

A better way to start is to put yourself in the shoes of an audience member and ask yourself, "If I am in the audience (and not the expert), what content would be most important to me, right now?" For instance, if you are an accountant, you are most concerned with balancing the books, but if you are delivering a financial presentation to the C-level executives, they aren't really concerned about the numbers themselves; they are more concerned about how the numbers relate to profit and trends. If you're delivering the presentation to the sales team, they are more concerned about revenue and bonuses. If you are delivering the presentation to the board of directors, they are more concerned about shareholder equity and retained earnings. If you are delivering the presentation to frontline managers, they are more concerned with costs and expenses. None of these audiences are concerned with the balance sheet, debits, credits, or any of the data that the accountant wants to deliver. They are concerned with how the data affect their day-to-day lives.

Think of designing your presentations like choosing a birthday gift. I love wine. I love to unwind at the end of the day with a glass of fine Pinot Grigio. However, my wife, although she likes wine as well, gets a headache if she drinks more than one glass. So a wine-of-the-month club membership is a great gift for me, but not so great for my wife. Think of designing your presentations the same way. Stop focusing on yourself and what you want and focus more on what the audience really wants.

About 10 years ago, I was working with an architecture firm that was bidding on a contract with the University of Texas in Austin. The university was adding a high-tech microbiology building to its campus, and the committee members were torn between adding something modern and edgy and keeping with the historic culture of the campus. I arrived at the university a couple of days before the presentation, and the team assembled by the architecture firm had already identified the key concepts that they wanted to cover.

The first point in the presentation was "Our Experience with University Architecture." It took me the better part of an hour to convince the team that although their experience was important, the university didn't really care about how successful they had been in the past. The university was more concerned about keeping its historic culture. After a pretty intense discussion, one of the architects decided to take a walk on campus to get some ideas, and while he was walking, he sketched some of the buildings that were already on campus. He made these sketches just so he could get some ideas and better understand the campus. For the next couple of hours, the team went over the sketches and identified what key aspects they wanted to "copy" and add into the new high-tech building.

When the team spoke to the committee, they began their presentation just like everyone else, with a couple of PowerPoint slides. However, after a few traditional slides, they inserted a blank slide that the team used as a spotlight for the sketches that the architect had created. He glued to sketches to a board and placed the boards on a tripod in front of the "spotlight." He pointed out the key aspects of the historic culture in the old buildings that he wanted to preserve in the new buildings. With every new board that he showed, the committee members physically moved toward the presenter in their seats. The committee loved the presentation and awarded the contract to our team within 30 minutes of the conclusion of the last presentation (a record).

After the presentation, one of the committee members approached the lead presenter and thanked him. He told us that every other one of the competitors had spent most of their time proving how great they were, but our team spent most of our time focusing on what the committee was most interested in. He said, "We all assumed that the people who invited each of the presenting companies did a good job, so if you were invited to present, we all assumed that you were qualified." The committee liked our company, because the presenters focused on the university and its wants and needs.

So when you start with your audience in mind, designing the presentation gets much, much *easier!*

TITLE

Design Your Title Based on the Main "Want" of the Audience

Now that we are thinking like the audience, let's design the title based on what the audience really wants. For instance, in the accounting example that I mentioned earlier, most presenters would create a title like "Fourth-Quarter Financials." (Trust me . . . even accountants don't want to listen to this talk.)

Going back through the different audiences, if the presentation is being delivered to the C-level executives who are interested in profit, a better title would be "Profit Increased by 2.5% in the Fourth Quarter."

The title for the sales team might be something like "Although Unit Sales Decreased in the Fourth Quarter, Total Revenue and Bonuses Increased."

For the board of directors, "A Small Increase in Profit Led to the First Dividend in the Last Three Quarters" might be a better title.

And for the frontline managers, the title might read "Revenue Increased This Quarter, but Rising Costs Led to Just a Small Increase in Profit."

As the audience changes, the topic title (and the content) will change as well. The more specific the audience is, the easier it is to create the title, because the title is designed for just what the audience wants most out of the presentation. If the audience gets broader, designing the title (and the presentation) becomes more difficult. For instance, if the person delivering the financial presentation mentioned previously was designing the presentation for a company-wide meeting and each of these groups would be attending, then the title might be something like "Although Revenue Increased Last Quarter, Profit Was Slight Because of Increasing Costs."

Think of designing the title like picking out a car. In the early days of car manufacturing, choices were limited, and as a result, so was the market. In Henry Ford's autobiography, Ford wrote, "Any customer can have a car painted any color that he wants so long as it is black."

In today's world, though, a black car that carries only four passengers and tops out at 35 miles per hour won't go over very well. Neither will a monolithic presentation designed for everyone.

The real key to creating a great title is to think entirely of the audience before you design it. Do this, and you'll end up with a much better presentation.

CREATE A CONCISE PRESENTATION BASED ON THE NEEDS/WANTS OF THE AUDIENCE

One of the things that I do in the first hour of the Fearless Presentations public speaking classes is give the participants 10 quick tips that will help them reduce public speaking fear almost immediately. Now, I feel like I'm a pretty good speaker. I use lots of examples and stories, I'm very enthusiastic, and I use some fun audience participation as well. I typically spend about 45 minutes giving these tips, so I cover each tip very thoroughly. However, I do this really to make a point, because as good as I am, within about 30 seconds after I give the last tip, I have the group take a quiz to see how many of the 10 tips they can remember. I've given that same test to more than 500 different classes, and the average number of items that people remember (just 30 seconds after the presentation ends) is only about three to five points—and that is with a pretty entertaining delivery.

The reason for this exercise is to prove a very, very important point about how people retain information. Here I am, a professional speaker, and I know my content inside and out. I'm very confident in my delivery, I make the content fun to listen to, and the audience is very active in the process—and most people in the audience will still remember only three to five things that I say. So if that's the case, if I really want to make my presentation impactful, I'll make the content very concise and cover only a few points per presentation.

18

TITLE

1)

2)

3)

4)

5)

Most Presenters Try to Cover Way Too Much Information in Way Too Little Time

If you spend an entire hour presenting on just one key concept—one key point—there is a really good chance that most people in your audience will remember your key point (at least for a short period of time). If you spend an entire hour covering two key points, your audience will have a 50 percent chance of remembering either (not both) of your key points. So, what that means is that an hour or so after your presentation, if you randomly asked people in your audience to name one of your key points, every other person will likely stare at you blankly. If you add a third point, the retention drops to just 25 percent. With four points, it drops to less than 10 percent. And if you add a fifth point, only about 1 percent of your audience will remember *anything* that you say.

Quick! Think of the last presentation you heard at the office. Do you even remember what the topic was? If so, do you remember any of the bullet points?

I know what you are thinking. Wait a minute. If retention is so low, then why bother?

I'm not trying to discourage you, but I am trying to get you to face reality. If you design presentations the way that most people design presentations, your audience will likely not remember a lot of your content, and even worse, they probably won't like your delivery.

However, if you follow the structure that I outline in the rest of this chapter, you will dramatically increase the retention from your audience. In fact, when class members finish our Fearless Presentations class, every class member delivers a final presentation where he or she puts everything that we cover in the class into practice. It's amazing how much of each person's content the class members remember at the conclusion of the talk. Not only do they remember the key points and titles, but they also remember names, dates, numbers, and many minute details that typically shock them.

So don't get discouraged. Just follow these tips:

Once you have that well-written and well-defined title, keep thinking like the audience. Ask yourself, "If I were sitting in one of these seats for an hour, and I walked away with only one key concept about this topic, what would be the absolute, number-one, most important thing that I'd need to know or remember? What would make it worth my while sitting through this presentation?" Whatever that number-one, most important concept is, make it your number-one key point (your first bullet point).

Once you have that most important concept, assume that the audience absolutely understands that concept very thoroughly. What would be the second most important key point that the audience would need to know? That point becomes bullet point number two.

Keep going until you get three, four, or five points. Just as an FYI, a well-designed three-point talk will take anywhere from 10 to 30 minutes to deliver. A five-point talk is typically most appropriate for about an hourlong presentation.

The logic of using this type of structure is pretty sound. If your audience is likely to remember only a few key concepts, then why not spend most of your time on the absolute most important things that they need to know? By the way, on a scale of "most important," when you identify the most important concept and work your way down the ladder, by the time you get to the fifth and sixth most important items, they will greatly pale in comparison to the number-one most important thing.

The next time you buy something, take a look at all of the options in front of you. Start rating your options from your favorite to your least favorite. Once you get to the sixth favorite, compare it with your top pick. Is there any real comparison? I went shopping for a suit a few weeks back, and I gave the salesperson a general idea of what I was looking for. As the two of us walked through the store, when I saw a suit that I liked, the salesman would pull it out and hang it near the mirror. When we got to about five suits, I went back and looked at each again. I was quickly able to rule out a couple, because compared with my top choices, they just didn't measure up. Eventually, I tried on a couple of suits and made my choice. As the salesperson was taking my measurements for the alterations, I stood looking at myself in the mirror admiring the new suit. Of course, the two suits that I had quickly excluded were still hanging there. As I looked at them, I wondered why I had even chosen them as finalists.

Your audience does the same thing. They may politely listen to all of your long list of 10, 15, 25, or even 50 bullet points, but somewhere along the way, they will disregard whatever they don't feel is important for them at the time. If you are delivering a bunch of bullet points, this filtering process will likely start to occur fairly early in the presentation. The more focused your presentation—meaning, the fewer key points that you cover—the more likely your audience will stay in tune with you and remember what you present to them.

Once you have your title and your key points, the final step in creating your outline is to make each of your key points really audience focused. The very crass, but effective, test that I like to use is the "Do I give a flip?" test. Meaning, if you were sitting in the audience and you saw this title and key points listed on a slide, would you say, "Cool, I can't wait to hear this," or would you likely say, "I hope this doesn't put me to sleep"? If it is the former, then you are on the right track. If it is the latter, you might want to change things around a little.

MAKE YOUR BULLETS COMPLETE STATEMENTS

An easy correction that you can make is to look at your bullet points and make sure that what you have written is a complete thought or a complete sentence, versus just a couple of words. When we put only a couple of words down, it might be a good cheat sheet or refresher for us, but the words are not likely to explain to the audience what you are going to cover. Remember that an effective bullet point is a visual aid for your audience, not a cheat sheet for the presenter. The audience should be able to look at your title and key points and know exactly what you presentation will cover and what your conclusion is.

For instance, if my bullet is "Closing Ratios," then the audience will have more questions than answers. What about closing ratios? Were they up? Were they down? Did something change? Why are we talking about them? A better bullet point might be, "Our New Salespeople Are Closing Only about Half as Many Sales as Our More Seasoned Salespeople, So We Need Better Initial Sales Training."

I know it's long and cumbersome, but when your audience reads it, they know exactly what your point is. (By the way, you'll shorten it down when you create your slide, but for now, your bullet points must make a full and complete statement.)

AVOID ASKING QUESTIONS IN YOUR BULLETS

Another good tip related to designing your bullets is to use statements, not questions. For example, if we made the bullet point, "How Do Closing Ratios for New People Compare with Those for Seasoned Salespeople?" the audience would be saying, "Well, I don't know. Why are you asking me? I thought you were the expert." So instead of asking the audience a bullet point, tell them what you are covering.

Your audience should be able to look at a single slide with your title and three to five well-designed key points and be able to quickly understand what your presentation is about, what concepts you will cover, and why they really need to listen. To do that, follow the steps that we've covered:

Step 1—Audience: Focus on what the audience wants, not what you want to tell them.

Step 2—Title: Create a title that covers the content the audience really needs or wants.

Step 3—Key Points: Limit your content to three, four, or five of the absolute most important concepts that the audience needs to know. Make your bullets complete thoughts based on the wants and needs of the audience.

Once you have your bullet points designed, a good test for each bullet point is to ask yourself, "Can I prove this?" If the answer is "yes," then you probably have a good bullet point. If the answer is "no," then you probably don't have a complete statement. Finish your thought, and the rest of the design process will be much easier.

PROVE TO THE AUDIENCE THAT YOUR BULLET POINTS ARE TRUE

Now that you have a well-designed outline of your speech, let's put some meat on the bones. When you start adding in the content to your presentation, pretend you are an attorney and are presenting your case to the jury. To prove your case, you are going to need evidence. One of the best types of evidence in a presentation is eyewitness testimony, and unlike an attorney, you can often be your own best witness.

First-person stories and examples are a fast and easy way to not only prove your points but also to make your presentations more entertaining and easier to deliver. For instance, if sales were up by 2 percent, the statistic itself will be quickly forgotten (by both the audience and the presenter), but the story behind the statistic is probably pretty interesting. One statistic is fairly easy for the presenter to remember, but what if the presenter also had to remember that first-time customers decreased by 4 percent, existing customers bought 12 percent more product, we lost two big clients through attrition, our prices increased by 8 percent this quarter, our new salespeople were closing only 12 percent of their leads, and more seasoned salespeople closed 25 percent of their leads? What most presenters will do is create a slide that looks like this:

Fourth-Quarter Financials

- Sales Up 2%
- First-time Customers Decreased by 4%
- Revenue from Existing Customers Up 12%

- Attrition Is Still Occurring
- Manufacturing Costs Increased by 10%
- Prices Increased by 8%
- New Salespeople Closed 12% of Leads
- Seasoned Salespeople Closed 25% of Leads

Of course, the way that the presenter would deliver this information is by reading a bullet, adding a little clarity for the point, and clicking to move on to the next point . . . to be repeated again and again. This type of delivery is very hard on both the presenter and the audience. The audience will forget most of the data almost immediately and will be tuning in and out throughout the presentation out of sheer boredom.

Let's use the bullet point that we created earlier, but use examples and stories to explain the data:

- Our New Salespeople Are Closing Only about Half as Many New Sales as Our More Seasoned Salespeople.

"In October, I got a phone call from Robert in procurement telling me that the cost of copper had gone up pretty significantly in the last quarter, which made our manufacturing costs increase by almost 10 percent. Since this was the third time that costs had increased in the past couple of years, we knew that we'd have to increase our sales price—at least a little. So I called the vice president of sales, and he and I agreed that a modest 8 percent increase in price wouldn't recoup our entire added expense, but it would keep us from going further into the hole.

"So, we had our sales reps call all of their existing customers and explain the situation. The initial fallout was pretty quick. Nash and Company and Singer, Inc. each pulled their orders right away, which hurt quite a bit. However, as our sales team called more and more of its clients, they began to get better and better at explaining what is happening in the industry. So, we ended up losing only those two clients. The salespeople who had the most existing clients got the most practice making these phone calls, so as they began receiving new requests for quotes, they ended up closing about 25 percent of their new leads. The younger and new salespeople had more trouble, though. They closed only about half as many new leads as the more seasoned salespeople did. As a result, we had a slight decrease in new sales. Overall, though, the price increase allowed us to generate about 12 percent more revenue from our existing clients and about a 2 percent increase in total sales.

"My suggestion would be to get the seasoned salespeople to work a little with the new guys to help them have better conversations with new potential clients. If we can get the new salespeople to close as many new leads as our other folks, we should see an increase in both units sold and revenue."

You see, in the first example, the statistics were the bullets. The data were the presentation . . . or rather the presentation was the data. In the second example, with a more well-defined bullet point, the data become the proof that the bullet point is true. What's even better is that when the presenter delivers the second presentation, since the presenter was an eyewitness to everything that occurred in the story, all the presenter has to do is replay the video in his or her head and tell the audience what he or she sees in the video. If the presenter forgets a few details or leaves a few of the details out, it's really no big deal, because the story itself is proof of the conclusion— that we need to train the new salespeople.

Interestingly, when we hear data in a story format, we tend to remember it a lot better. Let's test it. Without looking at the pre- ceding story again, what percentage of new leads did the seasoned salespeople close? Try to test yourself on a few more of the details and see how many you can recall.

ONCE YOU HAVE A GOOD OUTLINE, USE STORIES TO PROVE YOUR POINTS

If you want to design very compelling presentations very quickly, start with a good audience-focused title, create three to five points covering the most important topics, and use stories or examples to prove that each point is true. If you follow these simple steps, designing and delivering great presentations will be very easy and your audience will love you.

CHAPTER 3

Add Tremendous Impact to Your Presentations and Become the "Go-To" Expert

"If everyone is thinking alike, then somebody isn't thinking."
—George Patton

If you want to be seen as the expert, then you can't just do what everyone else is doing.

We already know that if we run our businesses just like everyone else, we will quickly be swallowed up by the competition. But when we design our presentations, we often totally disregard our own advice. Be different. Stand out from the crowd. Do something to help your audience better understand your content, but also make your presentation more memorable. When you finish your presentation, you want your audience to be thinking, "Man, that presenter really knows his [or her] stuff."

Any magician will tell you that the magic tricks themselves are fairly irrelevant to the success of the magician or the show. What's more important is what they call the patter. The patter is the running commentary of the magician that accompanies the trick. It is the showmanship that temporarily gets the audience's attention off the trick and focused somewhere else. Magicians like Penn and Teller will use jokes and funny stories as their patter. Magicians like David Copperfield or Siegfried and Roy rarely use verbal patter, but instead rely on stunning visuals like a pretty assistant dressed very seductively or albino tigers. Regardless of what type of patter a magician uses, it's the patter that creates the show. Most of these magicians are going to perform very similar illusions, but each creates a distinct show with their showmanship.

When you design and deliver your presentations, you are likely to be delivering material that is somewhat, if not exactly, what your competitors are delivering. So you need to add your own "patter" to the presentation to make it really come alive.

Avoid the long lectures filled with pages and pages of PowerPoint slides and endless bullet points. That's what everyone else is doing, and it's boring. Instead, use some of these 10 presentation secrets to add impact to your speeches.

IMPACT IDEA #1: STORIES AND EXAMPLES ARE YOUR ACE IN THE HOLE

I know we covered stories and examples in the previous chapter, but it bears repeating. The stories and examples that you use are entirely unique to *you*. No one can relate your own personal experiences or your expertise better than you can, so when you use personal experiences where you were the eyewitness, you are creating a presentation that is unique and different and that builds your credibility as the expert.

Years ago, I interviewed with a company to do some private presentation coaching for a group of presenters. I met with one of their project managers in a boardroom in downtown Houston to discuss the possibility of doing the project. I asked him a few questions about what kind of challenges the company's presenters were having, and he explained to me that his company often locked in contracts with school districts and universities by having the actual people who would be working with the clients (the engineers, architects, project managers, and so on) deliver the sales presentation, which they called the interview. The clients didn't want professional salespeople delivering the presentations. They wanted to meet the people with whom they would actually be working for the next 3 to 5 years. Most of the speakers were really nervous, because these contracts might total hundreds of millions of dollars. If they did well, everyone was busy for years, but if they didn't do well, they could lose out on a lot of work and a lot of money. No pressure, right?

At the time, I had spent the better part of 12 years coaching presenters, and for the past 3 years, the Associated General Contractors of America had been my largest client. This meant I had worked with most of the top commercial builders and engineering firms in the area. As a result, I was highly qualified for the job. But I knew that although quoting all my expertise and success might have made an impression, it probably wouldn't seal the deal.

However, one of these engineering firms that I had worked with a couple of years prior had sent all of its top executives to my class. At the time they had a corporate goal that they called Route 66, where they wanted to create $66 million dollars in contracts by the end of the year. When the class started, the company was at only about 80 percent of where they needed to be to hit the goal. During the class, though, these executives worked on a few projects to help them close more big contracts, and they made up ground very quickly. In fact, they ended up hitting the goal by late November. During this interview with the project manager, I relayed some of the stories about what I did to help the other company accomplish their Route 66 goal. By the time I finished the second success story, the project manager left the room and came back with one of the company's senior vice presidents. By the time I finished the third, the chairman of the board had joined us. The vice president looked at the chairman and said, "I think this is our guy. He really knows our industry."

Keep in mind that I had never in my life built or managed the building of a big skyscraper, and I knew very little about the day-to-day operations of a big engineering firm or construction firm. However, my experience working with people in the industry and helping them succeed made me the expert.

My story—that is, my experience—about just one of the many successes that I had accomplished proved that I was the expert.

IMPACT IDEA #2: AUDIENCE PARTICIPATION GAINS CONSENSUS

Many presenters are deathly afraid of asking for audience participation, and others actually misuse questions in a way that alienates the audience. But audience participation questions are a fantastic way to both gain a consensus from your audience and use the expertise in your audience to prove your point. So if you avoid using them, you are missing out on a tremendous tool in your tool belt. Since questions to the audience can be tricky, though, let's first cover some of the big mistakes that presenters make when trying to get the audience to participate and discuss how to avoid them.

- **Rhetorical Audience Participation:** Rhetorical questions can be strange for the audience. They serve almost no purpose in a presentation, so you want to avoid rhetorical questions in most cases. An example is a question that almost everyone will answer the same way, such as, "We've all learned to drive a car, right?"

or "How many of you have ever had a bad experience at a restaurant?" The questions will seem so elementary that people in the audience will be thinking, "Does he really want me to answer that?" There is also the potential to sound like you are trying to manipulate the audience. For instance, a question like, "You do want your family to be secure if something ever happens to you, right?" can push people's buttons. The best course of action is to avoid rhetorical questions. One of my early mentors in presentation training once told me, "Never ask a question unless you really want people to answer it"; it is has always been a pretty good rule.

- **Yes/No Questions:** Remember that the purpose of a good audience participation question is to get them involved and to gain a consensus. Yes/no questions have the opposite effect. Some people will answer yes and some will answer no, so by definition, if you ask one of these questions, you will end up dividing the audience. (Plus, there's not really a lot of interaction.) Although there are a few situations in which these types of questions will be beneficial, it's best to avoid them.

- **Open-Ended Questions with Multiple Correct Answers:** The best type of audience participation questions are those that (1) are open ended so that the audience really gets to provide input, (2) are opinion-based so that they have multiple correct answers, and (3) are helpful in proving your bullet point. If the question has only one answer, then you have only two possible outcomes. Either one single person will get the answer so you won't really gain much of a consensus, or no one will get the correct answer and you will make the audience feel stupid. Neither of these outcomes is great. However, if the answers are opinion-based, then any answer that the audience gives you will serve you well.

I have to admit that designing really good questions to ask your audience was very challenging when I first started coaching presentation classes, but after I had taught about 50 different classes, I noticed a pattern. Once I noticed it, I began to relay this secret to future classes and coming up with great questions has been a snap. I've taught a lot of public speaking classes, I've read a ton of presentation skill books, and I communicate with some of the top trainers in the world, but I've never come across this secret that I'm about to share with you anywhere else. In fact, it was purely by accident that I uncovered it, but it works every time.

If you design a really good key point (bullet point) like we covered in the previous chapter and it passes both the "Do I give a flip?" test and the "Can I prove this?" test, then you can pretty much just put a question mark at the end of the statement and ask it of the audience versus telling them.

For instance, the statement that we created in the last chapter was, "Our New Salespeople Are Closing Only about Half as Many New

Sales as Our More Seasoned Salespeople." And our conclusion was that we needed more training for the new salespeople. Instead of telling the story up front with all of the statistics, you might start with a question like, "Why do you suppose that our new salespeople are having a tougher time closing new leads than our more seasoned salespeople?" Your audience will likely give you a number of different possible answers, ranging from "They need better training" to "The seasoned salespeople are more confident" to "The seasoned salespeople have more knowledge about their products"—and probably many, many more. Regardless of what the audience tells you in response to your question, they are telling you *why* we need to train the new salespeople better. The new salespeople need more training, they need to be more confident, and they need to know their products better. All three of these led them to the conclusion that you wanted them to draw in the first place.

This process works so well that I have given entire speeches using only this technique—and achieved phenomenal results. Back when I was first starting out, I got a call from an event organizer for the Fort Worth Petroleum Accountants Association wondering if I could fill in for a guest speaker who bailed on them less than 24 hours before the presentation. I was happy to and honored that they would think of me, so I accepted the invitation. When I brought up a few possible topics that I could cover, she paused and sucked in a deep breath and said, "Well, that's the big problem. The agenda is already set, and all of the brochures have already been printed. Would it be possible for you to deliver your presentation on the topic that we already have on the agenda?" I had to think quickly, because I knew that if I didn't, she would likely find someone else to speak, and at the time, I really needed the honorarium. I reluctantly agreed to deliver the presentation.

I did some quick research on the topic, which was a highly technical accounting talk specific to oil and gas law. I made up a slide with three bullet points on it. Now, I took accounting in college, and

I actually enjoyed the class, but I couldn't tell you today the difference between a debit and a credit. And I actually began the speech by relaying that fact. But I followed up with, "However, we have a vast expertise in this room that I'd like to pull from, so this will be fairly interactive." I made the first statement in the form of a question, and I just held my arms out, with open palms facing the audience. Very quickly, a young man about five tables back to my right chimed in with an answer. I summarized what the man said so that the audience could hear the whole response, and very quickly, I had a few people raise their hands on the left side of the room. After six or seven people responded, I quickly summarized all of the responses and then moved on to point number two and did the same thing.

Keep in mind that during most of these responses, I had no clue what they were talking about, but the more the audience answered my questions, the more I saw heads nodding and people sitting on the edge of their seats. By the time I asked the third question, there were dozens of people participating and a deep discussion was occurring.

Just like with the prior questions, I concluded by summarizing what the audience told me about each point. I received a very loud and enthusiastic applause when I finished, and after the presentation, I had no fewer than six people come tell me that this was the best presentation they had watched in this meeting for the past few years. One of them even came up to me and said, "Thank you so much for explaining this to us. I was really confused about this topic before you started speaking." I didn't have the heart to tell her that I was really confused about the topic after I stopped speaking.

A good open-ended audience participation question with lots of possible correct answers can work wonders for you if the topic you are delivering is controversial and you need the audience to agree on your conclusion or if the audience that you are speaking to is full of people who have as much or more expertise than you do.

Before we move on to the next impact idea, though, let's get some more practice designing good questions.

Let's say that you sell computer equipment or software, and one of the main benefits you offer customers is data storage at a secure "virtual" location. If your bullet point is

- Data Stored Off-Site

then it doesn't pass the "Do I give a flip?" test and will be difficult to turn into a question. So let's add a little to the bullet. The bullet point has to give the audience the result or the benefit, so let's alter it a little.

- Off-Site Data Storage Offers Instant Access from Any Location with Internet Access

Now it passes the test, and it's very easy to turn into a question, for example, "What kind of advantages would your employees have if they had instant access to your company data as long as they had Internet access?" If you are the software salesperson, would it really matter what answers the audience gives you? Not really, because any answer that they reply with will reinforce your conclusion—that they need their data stored at a secure virtual location.

Let's do one more. This time you are a financial planner, and you are trying to explain to your audience how it is even more important to diversify their portfolios in a recession.

- Diversification Is Important

Really? How? Why? Let's add to it again.

- Diversification Is Even More Important in a Recession to Minimize Risk

Your question might be, "In what ways might diversification be even more important in a recession?" or "In what ways could diversification help you minimize your risk of loss in a recession?"

Regardless of what question you end up with, be sure to practice the question with a friend or a group of people from your office. Attorneys always say, "Never ask a question that you don't already know the answer to"; this applies to presentation questions as well. If the answers that your friends or colleagues give you are not the answers that you were looking for, then change the question until you get the answers that you need.

The reason that I have spent so much time on this impact idea is that audience participation is something that most presenters have no clue how to do well, so many of them never even try. In doing so, they miss fantastic opportunities to persuade their audiences and win people over to their way of thinking. So when you master this impact idea, you will be inserting yourself into a very elite group of speakers.

IMPACT IDEA #3: ANALOGIES MAKE COMPLEX IDEAS EASY TO UNDERSTAND

When I was a kid, my parents took me to a store that had these posters that, at first glance, had a confusing array of strange icons and symbols. But when I put on a pair of red goggles, I could clearly see text that was hidden within the poster. Without the goggles, the poster was confusing, but with the goggles, the text was very clear—and it was so fun, that I quickly grabbed my little brother and brought him over to see my discovery. Analogies are similar to the poster goggles in that they make complex and confusing items within your speech more easily understood, and they often do it while adding energy and fun to your presentation.

An analogy is a comparison between two different things that highlights some point of similarity. The more different the things are that are being compared, the more fun the similarities are. Motivational speakers use analogies quite often, because the comparisons

Analogy

often elicit what I call a lightbulb effect from the audience—where the audience member has an instance of clarity and lights up. Here are a few examples of some famous analogies from history.

- **Paley's Watchmaker's Analogy:** In a book he wrote in 1802, William Paley compared creation and the existence of God with a watch. (Obviously no similarities, right?) His argument was that if you are walking through the forest and you come across a fine Swiss watch on the ground, the existence of the watch itself is proof of intelligent design, because there is no way that the watch could have come into existence naturally. His argument was that the solar system, life itself, gravity, and the forces at play here on Earth are all much more complex than a simple watch, so therefore, they couldn't have happened by accident.

- **Plato's Cave Analogy:** We are often told how the Socratic method is a great technique to use to persuade people, and Socrates's method of questioning opponents to get them to come to their own conclusions was effective. However, that same method that he used to win people over to his way of thinking also got him executed. Socrates was very temperate as he got older, and he used questions as a way to prove that people who were arguing with him were wrong. He'd basically keep asking the opponent questions until the opponent backed himself into a corner and had to admit that he was wrong. Apparently, Socrates did this one too many times, because he was ultimately sentenced to death for expressing his ideas against those of Athens. Plato's cave analogy was his attempt to explain why the people of Athens turned against his teacher. Plato explains that a man who is a slave is born in a cave and spends his entire life chained inside the cave. He has never had any experience in the open and has never even seen the sun except through a small opening that comes into the cave just a few hours every day. During these brief encounters with the outside world, he and his fellow slaves see shadows of birds flying on the cave wall, and the slave gets curious. One day, he breaks his chains and runs to the opening of the cave to see the outside world for the very first time. He sees real birds with feathers flying through the air and is amazed. So excited, he returns to his fellow slaves to explain what he has seen. Of course to the slaves, a bird is not a feathered, flying animal. It is a black spot that hovers on the rocks a few times a day. To them the shadow is their reality of what the bird is, and they think that the returning slave has gone mad. He is so uprooting their reality of what truth is that they have to stop him, and the mob kills him. Plato uses this story as an analogy to explain why his mentor was sentenced to death. To Plato, Socrates was enlightened but the people of Athens were too stuck in their reality to see it.

- **Forrest Gump's Mother:** "Life is like a box of chocolates. You never know what you are going to get." (Okay, I think that technically, it is a simile, but it's still pretty funny.)

- **Freud: The Unconscious Is Like the City of Rome:** Sigmund Freud was trying to explain how the unconscious mind never "loses" anything. He said that the unconscious is like the city of Rome, "a psychical entity with a similarly long, rich past, in which nothing that ever took shape has passed away, and in which all previous phases of development exist beside the most recent." What he was saying is that if you go to Rome today, you will see ancient buildings right alongside modern architecture. When a new building is planned, Romans don't just demolish the entire ancient city and start over. They insert the new with the old. Freud was saying that the unconscious mind works in a similar way. Once we establish our values and our belief systems, as new realizations come to us, they don't eliminate our older belief system all together. Thus our unconscious mind is like Rome.

As you can see, analogies can make some very technical and complex ideas much more relatable and easier to understand. (And they are fun as well.)

Earlier, I mentioned a point that a financial planner might make is that diversification is even more important in a recession because the market itself is risky but the potential for big rewards is also there. So if we wanted to create an analogy for this point, we might compare diversification in a recession to planting a garden in a harsh climate. You have a much better chance of success if you plant different crops than if you simply plant a single crop over and over.

One of the best (and most effective) analogies that I've ever heard in class was when another instructor and I were teaching a private class to Hewlett-Packard engineers. These folks were so smart and so technical that most of their presentations were very difficult for me and the other instructor to understand. They were apparently using English words, but when they put them together for us, it sounded like a foreign language. Then we got to the session on analogies; the clouds parted, and everything made sense.

(Keep in mind that this was almost a decade ago, so the technology involved seems ancient, although it was revolutionary at the time.) One of the engineers was involved in a project where the sales team had promised superfast server speeds, but when the team installed the new servers, the speeds were much slower than what the customer was promised. The engineer was trying to explain to the client who had just invested untold tens of thousands of dollars for the new equipment that in order to get to the speeds promised, he was going to have to invest an additional $30,000 to update the infrastructure associated with the new servers. When he originally gave this presentation before he attended our class, the client got incredibly irate and felt like he had just been conned, because the engineer had explained the problem to the client by saying, "The servers are working fine. You have an infrastructure problem, and if you want us to fix it, you'll need to pay us another $30,000." The client felt like the group had promised a result with a lower price point in order to increase the price later once they had committed the prior dollars.

Of course, when this engineer gave his presentation to us, the other instructor and I had the same perception. Then he explained it to us with an analogy. He said, "Picture yourself in a big city like Los Angeles, and you are on a superhighway with 32 lanes of traffic all going in the same direction with no on-ramps or off-ramps. All of the cars on the highway are flowing very smoothly. Then you hit the city limits, and this 32-lane highway changes to a two-lane gravel road. At that point, there is going to be a bottleneck, and the faster the flow of traffic prior to the bottleneck, the more severe the bottleneck will be." He said, "That is what is happening in your company data transfers. Our servers are the superhighway, but the moment that our servers get connected to your copper wires in the wall, it creates a bottleneck. The only way to fix it is to upgrade your old copper wires in the wall." (I know what some of you are thinking. What the heck is a copper wire?)

Once he used the analogy, the complicated issue became easier to understand. Analogies are a fun way to add energy to technical presentations, but they can also add those lightbulb moments to any presentation. Often they can add some much needed humor as well.

One final piece of caution, though. Analogies by themselves make terrible proof. They work incredibly well to add flavor to a point that you have already proved, but if you use only analogies as your evidence, then people will like your presentation, but after it's over and they think about what you said, they will question your veracity. Case in point, years ago, Stephen Hawking was being interviewed on a British morning show, and one of the reporters asked him, "What came before the big bang?" Now this is an excellent question because according to the theory, time was created at the moment that the big bang occurred, so what happened prior to it? Where did the matter that caused the explosion come from? These are questions that have plagued proponents of this theory since it was created. The logical answer is, "I don't really know," but apparently Hawking didn't want to admit that he didn't know, so he used a weak analogy to dismiss the question itself. He said that the question was meaningless, and it was like asking, "What is north of the North Pole?" He never answered the question. He just used an analogy to prove to the TV personality that the question was wrong, not him.

Analogies alone don't work very well as proof, but an analogy along with some substantive evidence, such as a personal experience, some research or data, an audience participation question, or some other type of proof, will win the audience over every time.

IMPACT IDEA #4: ANECDOTES—A FUN WAY TO ADD HUMOR AND RAPPORT

When Ronald Reagan died in 2004, one of the news agencies was interviewing a former speechwriter for him and the reporter asked, "They called Reagan 'The Great Communicator.' What was it about President Reagan that made him so relatable to so many people?" Without batting an eye, the speechwriter said, "President Reagan had an anecdote for everything."

Anecdotes are short stories that may be true or fictitious but that often have a funny ending or moral. One of my favorite professional speakers is Brian Tracy, and he is a master of the anecdote. In fact, he has a way of inserting anecdotes strategically between each of his teaching points. He was the keynote speaker at a speaking conference that I attended a couple of years ago, and he started his presentation by talking about how the people who adapt to change fastest have a strategic advantage over those who don't. During the explanation, he relayed a story about Albert Einstein in which Einstein and his teaching assistant were walking across campus after a final exam, and the teaching assistant questioned Einstein about why he had chosen to give the exact same questions on this test in the exact same order as he had given the previous class. The teaching assistant was concerned, because he knew that if word got out that the professor gave the same tests over and over, it might encourage cheating. After thinking for a couple of seconds, Einstein turned to the assistant and replied, "Yes, the questions might be the same, but since the last exam, the answers have changed."

Now, I'm not sure if that discussion ever took place, but it doesn't really matter. Einstein was on the forefront of breakthroughs in science, so the anecdote might have happened just the way that Tracy relayed it. Regardless, though, it helped Tracy add some humor into his speech and it also helped make the audience think a little differently about something that they probably took for granted.

The most important thing about anecdotes is the fact that when you get really good at delivering them, they help you build rapport with your audience, because they are fun and interesting.

One of the best places I've found anecdotes is in *Reader's Digest* magazines. This magazine often uses short humorous stories as separators and fillers after each of their stories. One of the teaching techniques that I use with new instructors when I train them is to have them choose a random anecdote from *Reader's Digest,* and then I find some way to insert it into a two-day class as a teaching point.

In one such instance, a new instructor was thumbing through a *Reader's Digest* and found a funny story that she wondered if we could fit into the class in some way. The story was about a teenage girl who was babysitting a four-year-old boy and went into the kitchen to make him a sandwich. As she was making the sandwich, she looked down by the trash can and saw the cat's litter box. It was really full (and quite smelly). With every stroke of the knife spreading the peanut butter, her stomach turned, until she finally couldn't take it anymore and knelt down to the floor and began scooping the waste into the trash can. Of course, since she was a teenager, she kind of grunted after every scoop. The little boy, hearing the commotion, walked in and looked over her shoulder as she continued. After the third or fourth scoop, she turned to the boy and said, "Does your mom ever do this?" The little boy looked back at her very confused and said, "No, the cat does."

I read the story and smiled. Now I just needed to find a way to insert it into the class. Since it happened to be a leadership class, we had a session in the third hour that covered listening skills. I added the story here as an example of how sometimes the words that people hear us say are often quite different from the words that we were trying to say. When I relayed the story, the audience all laughed. It worked pretty well.

Second-Person Story Anecdotes

Just as those eyewitness testimony stories that we covered early are great evidence for our bullet points, sometimes we need to rely on stories that other witnesses have experienced. For instance, if you are a manager or owner of a company and one of your associates relays a story to you about a success with a client, the story will likely have more validity if you quote the associate. Or if you are a salesperson and one of your engineers who installs the products or services that you sell relays a success story to you, then you'll have more credibility if you quote the engineer.

Whether you quote others or tell funny stories to make your points better, the main thing to remember about anecdotes and second-person stories is that unlike our own personal stories that are extremely easy to tell because we are relying on our own experience, anecdotes are much tougher. You really have to memorize them to have a good delivery. So be sure to practice these types of stories a few times before you deliver them to a real audience.

IMPACT IDEA #6: DEMONSTRATIONS

Demonstrations help audience members better understand processes or products, because they get to see the process or product in action. If you have ever gone to a state fair or trade show and walked around the vendor tables, they will often use demonstrations as a way to prove that their products work better than the competitors'. And although many infomercials are pretty annoying, they sell products well, primarily because of a demonstration. I was watching cable TV awhile back, and a commercial promoting a waterproof spray sealant came on. To prove how well the product worked, the spokesman replaced the bottom of a boat with a screen door that he sprayed with the sealant. Then he filmed himself sitting in the boat out on a lake. Now, I'm not sure that I'd ever buy this product, but it was certainly a memorable demonstration.

A couple of years ago, I had a salesman from the Riddell company go through the Fearless Presentations class, and he was pretty excited about a new technology that the company had created to make face masks on football helmets much easier to remove if a player received a head injury. The National Football League (NFL) and the National Collegiate Athletic Association (NCAA) typically don't have a lot of problems with this type of thing, because their players are often wearing fairly new and well-maintained equipment. However, on the high school level, helmets often get reused year after year, and water from sweat, rain, or sprinklers rusts the screws that hold on the face mask. If a player is injured, the rust makes it difficult to remove the helmet without cutting it off with a power tool. So Riddell created a new face mask that was held fast to the helmet without metal screws. It took a special tool shaped like a pencil to remove the face mask, but with the tool, the mask instantly pops off. To demonstrate the new technology, this salesperson had two of the biggest guys in the room come to the front of the class. One of them held the helmet while the other grabbed the attached face mask. The salesman asked the two men to try as hard as they could to remove the face mask; they pulled, tugged, twisted, pushed, and jerked the helmet and face mask without any success. He then pushed this pencil tool into a little slot and twisted it; the face mask instantly separated from the helmet.

It was a pretty effective demonstration, and the audience got a kick out of seeing their friends helping out with it.

If you are selling technical products like software, websites, applications, or machines (or if you are teaching people how to use any of these things), then a demonstration can be a very helpful way to add some clarity. Keep in mind, though, that if they just see you do it, they won't necessarily be comfortable doing it themselves. You'll have much better success if you have them walk through the demonstration on their own tablets or laptops. It's kind of like being a passenger in a car traveling to a new location and trying to return to that location at a later date. When you are the passenger, you don't pay much attention to all of the landmarks and surroundings. But when you are the driver, you do. So let your audience drive a little.

Although demonstrations are an effective way to teach a process or promote a product, there are other uses as well. One of the best demonstrations that I've ever had in class was from a line manager at a pharmaceutical company in Rhode Island, who added a little showmanship to his delivery. Before the presentation started, he secretly went to the coffee bar at the back of the room and palmed an open sugar packet. He hid the packet from us throughout his presentation, and about midway through, he asked the audience, "Do you know what a million dollars looks like in my industry?" Once he had our attention, he moved his hand toward the audience and let a sprinkling of sugar fall to the floor. He said, "If that much contaminant gets into one of our drug lines, we'll have to throw out a million dollars' worth of product." It was so dramatic that I got chills when he did it. It was a pretty cool way to make his point.

So if demonstrations are appropriate to your presentation, by all means use them.

IMPACT IDEA #6: QUOTE ANOTHER EXPERT TO INCREASE YOUR CREDIBILITY

If you can find another expert who agrees with your conclusion, then feel free to quote that expert. The more you can prove to your audience that your conclusion isn't an opinion but a fact that is agreed to by other experts, or even better, by other people in the audience, the more credibility your conclusion has.

Allan Pease is an author of 13 different books on presentation skills and body language, and one of the tips he gives to audiences to customize a presentation to each group is to "phone members of the audience in advance and ask them what they expect from your session and why they expect it. Then use their quotes throughout your presentation."

I often quote Jerry Seinfeld when I begin a seminar or class on presentation fear, because in one of his stand-up routines, he points out that the fear of public speaking is the number-one fear in

America, and the fear of death is number five. "So, you are five times as likely to want to be in the casket rather than up giving the eulogy."

Tom Peters, author of *In Search of Excellence*, often creates slides that have one quote per slide and uses the slide as a visual aid in the background as he tells a story or gives information. This is a great technique because he never actually refers to the quote, or if he does, it is a very quick reference. A big mistake I have seen far too often in a presentation is when a presenter puts a quote up on a slide and just says, "What does that quote mean to you?" About 25 percent of people in an audience will think this is a fantastic activity, but another 25 percent will not like the activity and are just too polite to say anything, and the final 50 percent will be very irritated by an activity like this. So if you use a quote as a visual aid, do like Tom Peters does and leave it unspoken.

IMPACT IDEA #7: SHOWMANSHIP ADDS DRAMA AND ENERGY TO THE PRESENTATION

Never disregard the entertainment value of a presentation. Most business presentations are really, really boring, so if you add just a little entertainment to your presentation, you will be remembered in a positive way. When I was a kid, I was fascinated by magic. To get enough money to buy a new magic trick, I used to scavenge for money by digging through the cushions of our couch and looking under the seats in my dad's car; I'd also collect Coke bottles to return for the deposit. What I figured out was that no matter how easy the trick looked when the guy in the store showed it to me, it was always much, much harder when I got home and tried it myself.

So when I started teaching leadership and management classes and I was looking for ways to "wow" the crowd, I went to my local magic store and asked the guy behind the counter for fool-proof magic tricks. One of the ones that they recommended was what they called the "solid water" trick, where water stays in a

Styrofoam cup even after you've poked a good-sized hole through it with a pencil. (The magician's code forbids me from telling you how the trick works, but trust me, it is so easy that a little kid could do it.) Once I practiced the trick a few times, I was excited to insert it into my class.

The session of class that I was teaching was on conflict resolution, and I was explaining to the class that if we respond to angry people in anger, it will always lead to an argument. In addition, when people are angry, they don't think very clearly, so it is difficult to get through to them with logic. First, you need to let them vent and diffuse the anger; then you might have a shot at persuading them. I pulled out my Styrofoam cup and started pouring water into it. Then I took my pencil and held it up to the full cup of water and said, "So when a person is angry, they will poke you and poke you (and I poked the cup twice—the second time the pencil went through both sides of the cup as a through and through) to try to get you to react to them." Of course, the audience was amazed when I pulled the pencil out of the cup and no water came out. I finished by saying, "Others will be amazed at your poise under pressure."

Sometimes, your visual aids themselves can be your showmanship. I was coaching a team of presenters who were competing against seven other companies for a big contract. Each competing company got 45 minutes to present, and there was a 15-minute intermission between each group for setup and takedown. Our team was going first, which is good, because if the team did well and set the bar high, the committee would be comparing everyone else to them throughout the rest of the day. The downside of being first, though, was that after hearing eight presentations in a little over 9 hours, the committee would be really burned out and would find it difficult to determine who said what. What often happens in these instances is that members of the committee really like specific groups, but when the members vote for the group that they liked, they accidentally end up voting for the wrong group.

So this group decided to use their visual aids as a memory aid. They created a 6-foot poster for each of their presenters, and at the top of each poster was a portrait of the speaker, in the middle were a few bullet points with projects that each had worked on similar to the project they were bidding on, and at the bottom of each poster were a few pictures of samples of each speaker's completed projects. As each person spoke, they used the posters as their visual aids by telling success stories about their past projects, noting how those projects related to the current project, and pointing to the bullet points and pictures related to each story. They gave such a great presentation that they were just ecstatic when it was over, and they raced from the room to congratulate one another. In their haste, they forgot their boards, so the next group who came in to present had to move the posters out of the way quickly so that they could set up their own visual aids. When they did, they placed the posters on the wall, facing out. The posters stayed there all day, so every new group who came in to present had their competitors' portraits staring at them. We couldn't have planned it better if we had done it on purpose. When the committee met at the end of the day to give their opinions about the presenters, I'm assuming that it was much easier for them to remember who the team was and what they had said because the visual aids were still in the room with them.

So be different and be creative, and you'll make a great impact on the audience.

IMPACT IDEA #8: A SAMPLE WILL GIVE THE AUDIENCE SOMETHING TANGIBLE TO REFER TO

A sample is something that the audience can see, touch, and feel. It might be a prop, a poster, a model, a product, or anything else that gives a visual representation of what you are covering in your presentation. A few weeks ago, I attended a company's convention where they had attendees from more than 100 different countries. The executive who ran the South American offices gave a short 15-minute presentation on his group, and at the end of the presentation, he had a team of people from his region distribute these individually wrapped chocolate candies from Brazil that were absolutely scrumptious. He got a big applause when he finished. A sample can be something as simple as a small parting gift, but whatever sample you give the audience, make sure that it helps you clarify your presentation.

I once had a chemical engineer in one of my presentations who had invented a type of plastic that could be fused together without any adhesives. He explained to us that there were unlimited applications for the product, but he had found a big niche in the medical field, because in order to do simple things like attach an IV to a patient, doctors and nurses have to use needles and adhesives to connect the IV bags to the patients and to hold the pieces in place. These adhesives will often introduce contaminants into the sterile environment. (Think about flypaper. Hang a piece of flypaper in your window, and in a couple of days, you will have all kinds of dirty objects in the glue.)

This new plastic technology eliminated the contaminant by eliminating the adhesive. This new plastic could be sterilized, and each piece could be attached to another piece and fused together without contamination. When he explained this to us, we logically understood what he was doing, but it was still pretty tough to visualize all of the different possible applications for the process—until he passed around a sample. He gave us a contact lens case that he created. The case had a washer in the lid that had been fused to the top of the cap. He explained to us that contact lens cases have a short lifetime, because what keeps the solution inside the case is a little washer in the cap that is attached by a type of glue. Once that glue starts to break down, the case is useless, because it will never again create a seal that will not leak. The sample that he passed around, though, had no adhesive, so it would never break down. He let us pick at the washer to try to get it to come out of the cap, but it was no use. His sample helped us understand something that was foreign to all of us just a few minutes prior.

Samples aren't always appropriate to a presentation, though. For instance, if you are giving a financial presentation, then a sample might not be a good choice. However, when they are appropriate, they can really help you sell your ideas. I once did some coaching for a team of presenters from the Southland Corporation, which owns and franchises out 7-11 convenience stores. One of the participants was a marketing manager who was rolling out a "healthy food" campaign. 7-11 has done a fantastic job over the past three or four decades of building some powerful brands. When you think about 7-11, you probably think about 32-ounce Big Gulp drinks and

Slurpees, as well as Big Bite Hot Dogs. Unfortunately, in the past 10 years or so, the market has changed pretty dramatically. The marketing manager told us that some of their stores sell more of a single brand of bottled water than all the soft drinks combined. The market wants healthier alternatives, so the company began rolling out deli-style sandwiches, salads, and fruit cups.

When she was delivering a practice presentation early on the second day of class, one of her bullet points was about how healthy and fresh their deli sandwiches were. I have to be completely honest. I was enjoying her presentation, but in the back of my mind, I was thinking, "I don't think I'd ever buy a deli sandwich from a convenience store when there is most likely a Subway right down the street." We took a lunch break, and while we were recessed, she went to one of her stores and bought one of these sandwiches. She also went across the street to a different store and bought a sandwich from a competitor. The one that she got from her store was beautiful. It was made with a really fresh bun and had bright green lettuce that was symmetrical all the way around the sandwich. She used the deli sandwich as a sample during her final presentation, and I realized that I had misjudged her and her store that morning. The sandwich looked really good. Then she pulled out the competitor's sandwich. It was one of those refrigerator sandwiches on plain sliced white bread and was cut into two triangles and shoved into a triangle box. She concluded by saying, "This is what you get at one of our competitor's places." It was brilliant.

A good sample can be very persuasive.

IMPACT IDEA #9: NAME DROP

Name drops are like quotes from experts without the actual quotes. For instance, when I mentioned earlier in the book that you want to limit your key bullet points to just three, four, or five, I'm not the only person who teaches presentation skills who believes that. Dale Carnegie was the father of modern presentation skills, and his books say the same thing. Toastmasters, PresentationSkills.com, and articles from *Presentation* magazine all concur. So if a number of experts agree with your conclusion, you can just list them.

Another type of name drop is a list of satisfied customers. For instance, my company, The Leader's Institute, works with more than 405 of the Fortune 500, including Exxon Mobil, Walmart, Chevron, and General Electric. Since those are four of the biggest companies in the United States, it gives me credibility to name drop them. "If those big companies trust him, I guess we can, too."

IMPACT IDEA #10: ANY VISUAL AID THAT IS NOT A POWERPOINT SLIDE

Never, never, never rely entirely on PowerPoint as your sole visual aid. From time to time, get away from your slide deck for something

a little more spontaneous. I picked up a handy trick from a friend who is also a professional speaker. After you have your slide show designed, pull out one of the slides. When you get to that point of the presentation, just go and write your bullet points from that deleted slide onto a whiteboard or flip chart. To the audience, this part of the presentation will seem fresh and spontaneous.

Another way to incorporate handwritten text is during the audience participation that we talked about earlier in this chapter. When you get responses from the audience, write their words on a board. It will help you to better incorporate their responses into your presentation, because you won't have to remember all of them individually. Also, the audience will like it much more because you are quoting them.

Instead of inserting a picture on a slide, you can get the picture, graph, or chart mounted onto a board fairly inexpensively now. A picture on a slide has a short life. Once you click the button, the picture goes away. But if you have a poster, you can keep it visible throughout your presentation.

A couple of years ago, a firm was competing to win a big five-year project to remodel old school buildings and build all the new schools in Denver, and they wanted to prove to the school board that they were qualified to do the project. The company had previously worked with more than 350 other school districts doing similar projects, so they listed all of the school district names on a movie credit–style slide where each name rolled from the bottom of the slide up to the top. It was pretty impressive, but it didn't make the kind of dramatic statement that they wanted. So we had one of their team members download a single picture from each of those 350 projects and create a poster for each of them. Because of a time crunch, they were able to get only about 125 created, but it was enough to create a pretty nice presence. When they set up the room, they lined each of the posters along the base of the wall in a U shape, and they had each poster tagged so that they could easily pull them out to reference them when they needed. As they began to present and tell their success stories, they would go to the appropriate poster, pull it out, and reference it during the story. When they were finished with that poster, they would place it back against the wall. They did this about six times during the presentation.

Because they pulled a single poster from the 125 posters for each story, the natural conclusion for the audience was, "Since they had a story for each of the posters that they pulled, they probably had a story for *all* of them."

Use your visuals well and avoid "death by PowerPoint."

USE AT LEAST ONE IMPACT IDEA FOR EACH BULLET

To create a knockout presentation that will cause your audience to realize just how much of an expert you are, take that skeleton of a presentation that we created in the previous chapter and add at least one *impact idea* to help you prove each of your bullet points. (I'd encourage you to add at least two or three if possible.)

The real beauty of a structure like this is that you don't have to memorize anything. You could create a single PowerPoint slide with your title and three to five key points, and then prepare two or three impact ideas for each point to prove that it is true. If you prepare three impact ideas, choose the best two of the three and use them in your presentation, keeping the third impact idea in your pocket as a fallback if you find the audience confused or if someone asks you a question during the presentation.

Regardless, if you stand in front of the group and forget one of your impact ideas, who cares? You really need only one to prove your point, and when you get really comfortable with the structure, you will likely begin to add new proof on the spur of the moment because you think of an even better way to prove the point on the fly.

Most people will start with their slide show and design a bullet point for every concept they want to tell the audience about, using the slides as a prompt so that they don't forget anything. Of course, the inevitable will happen. These presenters will either talk too long on every slide and begin to run out of time, or they will forget what they were going to say about one or more of the bullet points. It creates a mess to deliver and a mess for the audience to follow.

Instead, follow the simple structure I've outlined here. If you start to run out of time, just cut out a few of the details in one of your stories or skip an analogy. You really can't forget anything, because whatever you end up saying is exactly what the audience thinks you prepared.

You will always be seen as the *expert!*

CHAPTER 4

Putting Your Dynamic Presentation Together and Delivering It without Any Notes

"In making a speech one must study three points: first, the means of producing persuasion; second, the language; third the proper arrangement of the various parts of the speech."

—Aristotle

Let's review the process that we've covered so far. Step 1 is to create a title that is audience focused. Step 2 is to limit your key points to the top three, four, or five points. Step 3 is to insert proof or evidence that each of your points is true. When determining what evidence to include in your presentation, scan the list of 10 impact ideas and insert the ones that work best. All you really need is one piece of proof, but if you use a combination of two or three impact ideas, you will increase your credibility and become more persuasive.

Consider that each story, anecdote, or audience participation that you insert into your bullet points will take you between 1 and 2 minutes to deliver. So these three impact ideas should be the foundation that you use for each point. Use stories to convey facts and figures by telling the story behind the numbers. If you add in a quote or an analogy every once in a while, it should take your at least 3 minutes and maybe as long as 10 minutes to relay each of your key points. When you put it all together, your well-designed three-point talk will take between 10 and 30 minutes to deliver. If you design a five-point talk, it can last as little as 20 minutes or as long as an hour.

Why the big variance in time? It depends entirely on how detailed you are when you give your examples and stories and how many impact ideas you insert for each point. One of the things that I love about this structure is that it allows the presenter to hit his or her time allotment *exactly* every single time. Let's say that you have been given a 45-minute time slot, and just before you go on, the organizer of the meeting tells you that the earlier speakers went over, so they have to cut your time to 30 minutes. No problem. Just cut out an impact idea or two or give fewer details in a few of your stories. This structure puts you entirely in control of the timing of your presentation.

This aspect alone will put you into an elite group of presenters, because there are very few speakers out there—even professional speakers—who can hit an exact time frame, especially if the original time frame is changed on the fly. Most keynote speakers have a few standard speeches that they practice over and over until they are able to hit an exact time frame. Then they promote that 60-minute keynote without a whole lot of options. Because I use the structure just described, I have a distinct advantage over other speakers. If a client wants me to speak for 37 minutes, no problem. If a client needs me to speak for 74 minutes, no problem. If a client wants me to create an entirely new presentation based on another area of my expertise, no problem.

This flexible structure makes designing and delivering presentations unbelievably easy!

A few years ago, I was hired to deliver a keynote speech for an association of sales professionals in Chicago. Since I write presentations for a living and I use this structure, I knew that it would take me only a few minutes to design the presentation. I jotted down a few ideas on the plane ride to O'Hare Airport. Unfortunately, I'm embarrassed to say, six months prior to the presentation, when I was hired, the organizer and I had agreed on a topic that was different from the one that I prepared on the plane. As the organizer was calling the meeting to order, I looked on the agenda and realized my error—about 30 seconds before I was to be introduced. Sheer panic set in almost immediately, and my stomach churned. But as I was walking to the front, all I had to really think of on the spot were five key points related to the topic, which was actually pretty easy, because the topic was, "Five Key Things That You Can Do to Increase Sells in a Down Economy." I asked myself, "If this group walked away with only one key way to increase their sales in this economy, what would be most valuable for them?" And I had my first point. Then I asked myself, "What real-life story can I use to explain this point?" and I had my first piece of evidence. I literally designed the entire speech as I was giving it.

When the presentation was over, I received a huge round of applause and the organizer came up to me to tell me that of all of the presenters who had spoken to the group that year, my presentation was probably the best. He then hired me on the spot to deliver another presentation a year later. Interestingly, the speech I gave the next year was on "How to Design a Custom Presentation on the Fly," and I told them the self-deprecating story of what I had done the previous year as my introduction. Since many of the people in the audience the second year had also been there the prior year, they were amazed that I had created that entire speech the prior year while I was actually on stage giving the speech.

Now, I do *not* suggest that you design your presentations while you are in the process of giving them. I put myself in a terrible situation that could have cheated my audience and ruined my career, and it was entirely my own fault. However, because I had an expertise that is elusive to most speakers, I still succeeded.

If you master this process, you will become bulletproof (no pun intended) when you present your ideas to audiences.

WHAT HAPPENS WHEN YOU DON'T HAVE CONTROL OVER THE CONTENT?

Okay, we don't live in a Pollyanna society, and we sometimes have very little control over our content. For instance, one of the most difficult (and dangerous) presentations to deliver occurs when someone else designs a presentation and simply gives the presenter a slide deck. "Here is your presentation; now go deliver it." In addition, sometimes the meeting organizer will give you an agenda to follow. In many of the sales or interview presentations that I've referenced earlier, the prospective purchasers will send over a list of 10, 15, or 20 items that they want covered in the presentation, and they will often send this list to all of the presenters at the eleventh hour. A situation like this will limit your flexibility as the presenter. Sometimes, because of legal issues, presenters are asked to deliver only preapproved presentations or slide decks. Many big companies often create an approved presentation and then require that all of their salespeople use the same presentation. If you own a franchise or are a financial planner, realtor, or some other type of independent business owner working under a license, then you might be limited somewhat to what the parent organization has approved.

If you are forced to do it, can you give a 10-point talk in 15 minutes? Sure you can, but you need to manage your expectations. This type of presentation will likely be very difficult to deliver, and unless you are just incredibly charismatic and energetic, the presentation will be difficult to listen to as well. You also want to keep in mind that the audience members will likely not remember a lot of your content, because they will probably be overwhelmed. But you can do it.

Following are a few tips that can help you get better results.

BREAK UP THE BIG PRESENTATION INTO MULTIPLE PRESENTATIONS

If you have lots of content that you have to cover, then the best way to deliver all of your points is to break the presentation up into two or more different speeches. This is the technique that I used when I created my original leadership class, High Impact Leaders. I wrote a book called *28 Ways to Influence People & Gain "Buy-In"*, which identifies a single leadership principle for readers to apply every day for 28 consecutive days. It takes about 28 days to create a new habit, so this daily activity reinforces the leadership activity. The original High Impact Leaders class was composed of four individual seminars spaced a week apart, and in each session, we covered only the seven principles that the participants would be focusing on in the upcoming week. Then, a week later, we'd come back and cover the next seven for four consecutive weeks.

I know what you are thinking . . . "Wait a minute, Doug. You said that people will retain only three to five points, so why did you cover seven principles instead of five?" Well, because I had to. Just like the situations that you will find yourself in where you have to cover more than five points, I created one of these situations myself. However, I created a couple of additions to the program that made the retention of information much more solid. First, I created a desktop card file that looks like a set of business cards, and each card has one principle on the front of it. Participants would flip a card every day and get a daily reminder of the content (so, in effect, each day they were receiving a one-point talk).

The point, though, is that if I had given the audience the 28 principles in a single sitting, no one would remember any of them when the presentation was over. But when I broke the 28 principles into four different presentations, the retention went up exponentially.

INSERT A SHORT BREAK

Another option that you can use is to just insert a short break once you cover a few points. This is an easy option, because your break doesn't have to be a formal break. If you have 10 points, cover five of them, and then just say, "Hey, I've been speaking for a while, so let's just take a 3-minute stretch break so that you can refill your coffee. No need to leave the room, though, because we'll be taking a formal break in about 25 minutes."

The neat thing about this option is that you don't need to get an organizer's permission to do it, because it doesn't affect the agenda at all. However, if you are able, you could insert a formal break between your two parts and get much better results. For instance, if you are doing a breakout session with 10 items, then talk to the coordinator about giving you two consecutive breakout sessions and create a "Part 1" and a "Part 2."

GIVE PRINTED MATERIAL FOR ALL OF THE CONTENT BUT DELIVER ONLY A FEW OF THE POINTS

Years ago, I had a person from Hewlett-Packard (HP) attend one of my coaching sessions. She was an account rep, which basically means that she was one of the few top-level salespeople at her company who handle their really, really big accounts. These salespeople are the best-of-the-best in the companies (their Top Guns), and they got to this level because they are confident and because they are problem solvers.

After a few years, HP had a big problem. These high-level sales reps were creating presentations for their clients that were creative and on the cutting edge but that were sometimes contradictory and sometimes even different from what HP was distributing corporately. Out of necessity, HP made a corporate decision to create one big, all-encompassing preapproved slide deck that all of the account reps were required to use in their presentations. This slide deck included more than 100 slides, and most of the presentations that these sales reps delivered were less than an hour long. So when this account rep came to my class, she had a pretty big challenge.

What she ended up doing was printing off her slide deck as a "leave behind." Then based on the needs of the client that she was delivering to, she went to only 5 of the 100 slides during her delivery. At the beginning of her presentations, she would always say, "I know that you have a team of people who really like to see all of the details, so I am leaving a bound packet of information that I have indexed for you. But based on my discussions with you, it looks like you are most interested in . . ." She would then move to the slides that she had previously identified as the most important ones.

DELIVER EVERY POINT, BUT REINFORCE A FEW OF THE POINTS SEPARATELY

One of my favorite ways to cover a lot of data and still get the audience to remember some of the content is to deliver every point in a cursory fashion but then go back and reinforce three or so points more thoroughly. When I deliver the 10 impact ideas in my classes, I use this technique. I give the audience a handout with the 10 points (I don't have a slide with all 10 points), and I spend about 30 to 60 seconds covering each point. This allows me to get through all 10 impact ideas in about 15 minutes. Then I go back and cover the three most important points (typically stories, audience participation, and analogies) with a single slide that includes these most important points. I spend 30 minutes or longer on the three most important points, so, with the 15-minute overview, the session typically lasts just about 45 minutes. Because I reinforce the three main ideas at the conclusion of the presentation, the audience knows exactly what I believe are the most important of the items that I've covered.

This is the technique that I encourage presenters to use when they are conducting sales interviews or if they are delivering a short list presentation and the purchaser sends over a long list of items to cover at the eleventh hour. Answer or cover every item, but focus on the items that are going to be most important to the purchaser.

More on this in Chapter 8.

CHAPTER 5

PowerPoint Mistakes That Will Kill Your Chances of Doing Well and How to Avoid Them

"Why doesn't the fellow who says, "I'm no speechmaker," let it go at that instead of giving a demonstration?"

—Kin Hubbard

When we get calls and e-mails at work with questions about presentations, the most common topic that is referenced is Power-Point. In fact, when we first begin coaching new clients, they will frequently want to reduce their fear when giving PowerPoint presentations or will want to learn how to design PowerPoint presentations. They rarely call a presentation or a speech a presentation or a speech. They often refer to the presentation or speech as a PowerPoint presentation. Therein lies one of the biggest challenges that people have when they give business presentations. They forget that PowerPoint is just a visual aid. It is not the actual presentation.

So this chapter covers the top 10 mistakes that people make when they design and deliver PowerPoint presentations. Fortunately, most of these mistakes are created by the way that the presenters prepare their presentations, and simply by doing the things we've already outlined in this book, you'll eliminate most of these challenges automatically.

MISTAKE #1: TREATING POWERPOINT AS THE PRESENTATION AND NOT A VISUAL AID

The absolute biggest mistake that we make is designing a "PowerPoint Presentation" versus using PowerPoint as a visual aid for the "real presentation." Remember, a presentation is a verbal communication to your audience that may or may not use visual aids. PowerPoint is just *one* type of visual aid that can be used to further explain or clarify

your presentation. If you focus entirely on your visual aids without putting any emphasis on what you are actually saying, your presentation will tend to have a disconnected flow and will be difficult for the audience to follow. Instead, design your presentation and get good at delivering it first. Once you get good at delivering the presentation, then decide what visual aids you might be able to use to help you clarify your points.

The good news is that if design your presentation the way that we've outlined in the book, the PowerPoint slide show becomes very simple. In fact, you'll need only one slide for most presentations. At most, you might have six slides.

MISTAKE #2: USING TOO MANY POWERPOINT SLIDES

Another big mistake is creating too many slides and using them as a crutch to make sure that we don't forget anything in our

presentation. Speak . . . click . . . speak . . . click . . . speak . . . . click . . . is a very boring way to deliver a presentation; it makes the presenter look unprepared and uninformed about the topic. Only add a slide if the slide helps you better clarify your point.

Oddly enough, this mistake most often occurs because of the way we prepare a presentation, and it occurs whether you use PowerPoint or not (but it is much more obvious if you use PowerPoint). Most people prepare a presentation by trying to write down everything that they know about the topic. In the olden days (before 1996), we used to either write a presentation out longhand word-for-word or we'd write out a comprehensive outline. However, when we wrote the presentation out longhand and tried to read it, we could easily measure the amount of time it might take to deliver the presentation, so we'd start cutting content based on our time allotment. Since we knew it would be almost impossible to remember every single thing that we outlined, we would often trim the presentation down to a more manageable amount of content.

Then came PowerPoint. Now, because we had a digital cheat sheet, we no longer had to cut out content; we could make an unlimited number of slides, and we could fill up each slide with every minor concept that we had to cover. This led us to mistake #3.

MISTAKE #3: INCLUDING TOO MUCH CONTENT (TOO MANY BULLETS, CHARTS, AND GRAPHS)

Your slide deck should be a visual aid to help you explain your point, so if you put too much data on a slide (too much text, too many numbers, too many charts and graphs), you will overwhelm your audience, which results in them attempting to draw their own conclusions about the data. (Gasp! Is he saying that we can't use charts and graphs?) Your PowerPoint slide should convey a simple concept at a glance. A good rule is what we call 6 × 6, which means to limit your number of words per line to six and limit your number of lines to about six as well. That way, no matter how big or small your room is, your audience will be able to read your data, and it will be easy for the audience to instantly understand the concept you are communicating.

Again, the best way to avoid making this mistake is to use the three- to five-point talk as your format. If you do this, making slides for your slide deck is easy.

One quick tip, though: earlier in this book, I suggested that you create full and complete statements with your bullet points so that it is easier to come up with stories and audience participation questions. This is a preparation guide, which helps you, the presenter, clarify the

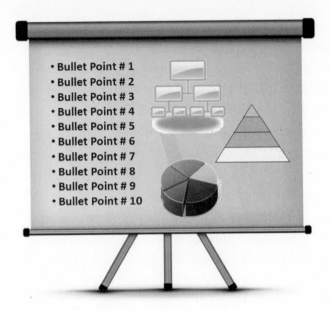

concepts that you want to get across to your audience. When you actually create a slide for the presentation, though, feel free to shorten the bullet point.

MISTAKE #4: USING TOO MUCH (FRIVOLOUS) ANIMATION

PowerPoint will do some really cool types of animation, but remember that if you animate something, it should help you clarify your point. Bullet points that fly in, spin around, make sounds, and blink are just distractions from your message. For the most part, the animation that PowerPoint calls "appear" should be your most frequently used animation type, so that when you click your handy transition button, the next bullet point just *appears*. If you want your audience to follow you step by step, you can reveal your bullets one at a time. However, you'll have more energy as a presenter if you just make your slide appear and physically move to your screen and point to your bullet point when you talk about it. You become the animation versus using the slide show.

This doesn't mean to avoid animation altogether. In fact, some of the best showmanship that I've ever experienced in presentations relied heavily on animation in a slide show. A few years back, one of my clients was competing to be the general contractor to build on an expansion to Fort Bliss in El Paso, Texas. The company had its animation team go to Google Maps and download a three-dimensional image of the terrain where the expansion was going to be, and the team created a movie starting with a digital picture of the bare land. A few seconds later, the roads leading to the area appeared. Next, the blacktop parking areas showed up. Eventually, buildings started to appear, along with fences and security towers. Finally, Jeeps and tanks started to drive in on the roads and park on the blacktops. At the end of the presentation, it was very easy for the Corps of Engineers, who was responsible for choosing the winning company, to see that this group knew exactly what it was doing. They could visually see the end product before it even existed in real life.

If the animation adds clarity to your conclusion, then by all means, use it. Otherwise, leave it out.

MISTAKE #5: INCLUDING TOO MANY BUSY CHARTS

(Gasp! He is saying not to use charts and graphs again!) For the most part, *charts, graphs, and pictures make terrible PowerPoint slides.* If the charts or graphs are simple, they can be judiciously used in a slide show. For instance, if you are showing total revenue trends for the past five years, you basically have five numbers, so a line graph will be very easy for your audience to understand. However, if you are graphing total revenue of five different divisions on a quarterly basis for each of your 10 major product lines, your graph will be way too

busy to understand in a slide. In that case, you'll get better results if you make a handout of the graph so that your audience can review the details. You can make a big poster of the graph if you need a visual aid for the group to follow, but in most cases, you can just use the handout itself as the visual aid.

About eight years ago, I was in San Antonio to do some personal coaching with a man who worked for a huge company. He was having a lot of trouble delivering presentations to his boss. His boss was a very analytical guy who had to send a spreadsheet with his district numbers to the corporate office every month. This boss would have each of his managers create a single PowerPoint slide on which the manager would insert a very detailed spreadsheet; the managers would then explain the spreadsheet in their meetings once every month. The boss did this because it allowed him to then copy the data from the spreadsheet in the slide show and paste it into his own spreadsheet, which made his task of creating a report for his boss much easier. To me, it just seemed really strange.

Obviously, neither my client nor I could really do anything about what his boss wanted from him, but I could help him with his presentation and visuals. I suggested that he send the boss his spreadsheet via e-mail, which should be much easier for him to copy and manipulate. In addition, I had him pick just the three most recent trends that he noticed each month in the numbers and design his presentation based on the changes or the trends versus trying to explain every single number every single month. (In reality, the boss really wanted only the numbers so that he could create his own report. The presentation was just a formality each month.)

MISTAKE #6: IMPROPERLY USING PICTURES

A picture is worth a 1,000 words—but only if the picture is important to your point. Often, we will look at a slide and think, "It

seems a little plain," so we stick a picture on the slide just to jazz it up a little. Although that is not, in itself, a terrible strategy, sometimes the pictures that we choose as decoration end up causing confusion because the audience wonders what the picture has to do with the point being made. A better way to use pictures as decorations is to set a small picture on the slide master so that it shows on every slide. That way, since the picture is always there, it doesn't cause confusion when the text changes. By the way, if you have a picture that adds clarity to your point, consider printing it as a poster. It will add much more impact when you can pick it up and show it to your audience.

More often than not, if the picture, chart, graph, or spreadsheet is important enough to put into a slide show, you'll likely get much better results if you include the visual aid as a handout or put it on a board.

MISTAKE #7: NOT PRACTICING YOUR PRESENTATION WITH THE SLIDE SHOW

Time is getting short, so you send your slide deck to marketing to jazz it up a little. They send you the final copy minutes before you go in front of the group. Everything is perfect in the slide show, but because you haven't practiced, your flow is off and you have to keep clicking to the next slide before you start to speak. It just makes you more nervous. If you have ever experienced this type of stress, then there is an easy fix. Don't wait until the last minute to design your slide show. Start preparing much earlier! Finish your slide deck early and practice with it once or twice; you will feel much more comfortable when you deliver the real presentation.

Just as an FYI, there is no need to overpractice if you have a well-designed presentation. A run-through with a coworker or friend is usually sufficient to help you deliver a confident presentation, but you need to practice the presentation with the visual aid in order to feel comfortable with it. When I train new instructors to teach my classes, it is really easy to tell whether they practiced with the slide show or not. If they practice without the slide show, they get really good at delivering the content but will often click to the next slide and show a visual aid for something that they just talked about. Practice at least once (and maybe a couple of times) with your slide show, and you'll do a better job in front of the real audience.

MISTAKE #8: SITTING DOWN TO DELIVER YOUR PRESENTATION

When folks get nervous speaking in front of a group, they will often sit down and make the screen that the slide show projects onto the focus of the presentation. The moment you sit down and start clicking slides, the PowerPoint slides become the authority in the room on the topic and you will lose a lot of credibility.

Your energy will also plummet when you sit down. Early on in my sales career, my sales manager suggested that when I'm talking to clients or potential clients on the phone that I stand up. He said that it would increase my "energy," which sounded kind of strange at the time, but because I started to get in the habit of standing while I'm on the phone, it's natural for me now. A few weeks back, a woman called to inquire about becoming a teacher for my company. I told her that I had just hired two new instructors in this quarter already, so I didn't have any positions open. But I told her that things change quickly, so she might want to keep in touch with me. The conversation lasted for all of about 3 minutes, and the last thing that she said was, "Oh, I will keep in touch. I love your energy. Just from what you've told me, your company sounds like a really fun place to work!" I hung up the phone a little confused, because all I had really told her was that I didn't have a job for her. How could that sound fun? Then it hit me that it wasn't really what I was saying, but more how I was saying it that she noticed. My energy was pretty high (as it normally is), and it came through across the phone line.

You can have a similar result when you deliver your presentations if you stand up and use your voice and gestures to portray energy.

MISTAKE #9: READ . . . CLICK . . . READ . . . CLICK . . .

If you are doing this one, then I hate to be the one to tell you this, but . . . you're boring! Sorry. I know that hurt, but it's true. The good news is that if you follow the prior guidelines, this one goes away automatically. So if you are experiencing this, go back and work on the earlier tips. You might also try inserting more examples and stories, as well as jazzing up your presentation with a few visual aids other than PowerPoint slides. Visual aids such as posters, samples, and props will make your presentation come to life.

MISTAKE #10: LETTING SOMEONE ELSE DESIGN YOUR SLIDE SHOW

This one is probably the guideline that will, most likely, be totally out of your control. Just realize that if someone else designs your PowerPoint slide deck, you will most likely have one or more of the earlier mistakes ingrained in it. You will also have a more difficult time delivering it and will be more nervous. To combat this, you'll need to practice your delivery a lot more than if you designed your own presentation, but it can be done. Over time, use the guidelines discussed in this chapter to influence the person or people who are designing your slide show.

Follow these simple guidelines, and your PowerPoint slides will help you better deliver more powerful presentations. Violate them, and you'll likely be more nervous and have a more difficult time delivering your presentation.

MORE POWERPOINT TIPS ARE AVAILABLE ONLINE

We receive numerous requests for fixing PowerPoint problems, so we created an online study course based on these mistakes and how to fix them. The course has 10 videos, one for each of these mistakes. And because you purchased this book, you can gain access to the tips for a big discount by visiting the website http://www .fearlesspresentations.com/how-to-do-a-powerpoint/ and entering the coupon code PSS100.

CHAPTER 6

Speaking Venues That Can Generate More Clients and Credibility

"It is not your customer's job to remember you. It is your obligation and responsibility to make sure they don't have the chance to forget you."
—Patricia Fripp

Now that you have an awesome presentation and you can create new and customized presentations on the fly in minutes versus hours or days, where do you go to speak? Following are 10 different speaking venues that will allow you to get additional practice speaking in front of groups and also generate new customers and clients along the way. When you are just starting out, choose a venue where the risk is low; then as you start to experience success delivering these presentations, increase your risk and the rewards will increase as well. The venues are listed based on their risk, so in your early stages, focus more time on the first few venues. As you get better and better, move down the list for a new challenge and bigger reward.

SOCIAL CLUBS, CHAMBERS OF COMMERCE, LIBRARIES, AND RECREATION CENTERS

These are the absolute easiest groups to appear before if you have information that is valuable to the members or customers. They are great locations to practice your presentations, but you aren't likely to generate a lot of customers from the groups. However, because influential people are often members of some of these organizations, the members may open doors to get you into a better speaking venue.

Social clubs include Rotary Clubs, Kiwanis clubs, Lions Clubs, Jaycees, Junior Leagues, and many other organizations where professional businesspeople congregate. Most of these clubs meet weekly and have a guest speaker for each meeting, so they are always looking for good speakers who can educate their members. Interestingly enough, your success generating new customers from these groups will depend primarily on the size of the city in which you live. If you live in a fairly small city, there will likely be one of these clubs where most of the influential people in the city are members. In bigger cities, many of these clubs have died out, so there may be dozens of each type of club with fairly low (and often aged) membership. The nice thing about doing presentations to these groups in larger cities, though, is that because every group needs a new speaker week after week after week, the elected officials who book speakers all talk to one another. This means one successful presentation will often lead to quite a few additional invitations to speak to other groups.

Chambers of commerce can sometimes be a better venue; however, it is much more difficult to get invited. Because the chambers of commerce represent every business in a community, they are very cautious about allowing individual business owners to speak before their members. However, they are always desperate for funds, so it is often very easy, for a small fee, to sponsor an event like a small-business breakfast or business card exchange. This sponsorship will often include 5 to 10 minutes to tell a little about your business. Just make sure that the chamber members themselves are potential customers for you. If you sell electronics to prime contractors, don't waste your time with chambers of commerce; although the prime contractors are members, representatives from these big companies never attend any of the events or meetings. If you sell things to small businesses or to individual businesspeople, though, this venue might be perfect for you.

Many city recreation centers, libraries, and community centers also often allow speakers to rent meeting rooms, and they publish their meetings in the monthly brochure. Accountants or financial planners often provide free or low-cost seminars in these venues to try to make connections with the local people.

Finally, local universities and junior colleges often have an adult education program where they offer seminars to the general public.

All these seminars are published in a course catalogue, so although you may not get paid much for presenting the seminar, you'll be listed as an instructor at that particular college, which has some advantages for marketing purposes.

LUNCH-N-LEARNS FOR SPECIFIC COMPANIES/GROUPS

Although you will have some cost involved in this venue, you can target your audience to a pinpoint. A Lunch-n-Learn is a short targeted seminar for a specific company or group that you want as a customer. For instance, drug reps often bring donuts or sandwiches to doctors' offices as a way to gather physicians and teach them about new drugs that are coming onto the market.

About 10 years ago, we came out with a new team-building event called Build-a-Bike, where companies hire us to lead a team activity for their group, which ends with the group assembling brand-new bikes for needy kids in their community. The combination of fun, high energy, team building, and philanthropy was a big hit, and it quickly became the most popular team-building activity that we offered. But early on, no one had ever heard of such a thing, so there was no demand for the event. My instructors and I visited the big hotels in each of our cities and brought lunch for the salespeople. While we were there, we told them about Build-a-Bike; within a few years it was an international sensation.

By the way, you don't have to sell to businesses to use this venue. If you run a gym, you might volunteer to teach a fitness class during lunch hour for a company's employees in exchange for them letting you hand out guest passes to your gym. One of my friends owns a boutique-style woman's clothing store, and she conducts free "Dress for Success" sessions at downtown law offices.

TELESEMINARS AND WEBINARS

It is actually pretty easy and very low risk to organize your own teleseminars or webinars, because with the technology today, both of these types of events can be offered at no cost to you. The reason this isn't listed higher, though, is twofold.

First, teleseminars and webinars are more complicated to deliver, because, for the most part, the presenter's voice is the main communication vehicle, whereas with in-person presentations, the presenter can use his or her gestures and body language as well. So it's kind of like trying to play a sport such as baseball with one hand tied behind your back. You can do it, but it's more complicated, so it takes more practice. (Jim Abbott made it to Major League Baseball as a pitcher even though he only had one hand.) However, once you get

good at regular presentations, teleseminars can be a great way to get more practice and challenge yourself in a different venue.

Second, to get people to attend your teleseminars, you need to have a message that people will drop everything to hear and a list of customers or potential customers big enough that you'd still attract a decent crowd even if only a small percentage of people attended.

A year or two ago, I received a cold call from a salesperson at a company that made promotional Internet movies for companies. At the time, I wasn't interested in purchasing a promotional Internet movie, but the salesperson invited me to attend a webinar that explained the process and showed some real examples of how the movies helped increase traffic to websites and convert more sales. It seemed harmless enough, and I began to see the possibilities with technology like this. I let the sales rep sign me up for the webinar and promptly forgot about it. The morning of the webinar, I got an e-mail from the company reminding me of the event, and since I had literally forgotten all about the call from the previous week, I clicked through to their website to remind myself. Of course, they had one of their own movies on their home page, so I watched it. I was starting to get impressed and interested in this process. A week before this webinar, I was a guy who knew nothing about this company, and I was not even close to becoming a suspect for their salespeople, much less a prospect. Now I was starting to become interested in this technology.

I logged into the webinar about 5 minutes ahead of time and heard folks introducing themselves and saying where they were from. Every time a new person came in, the system dinged; over the next 7 minutes or so, I kept hearing ding, ding, ding, ding. I guessed that there were probably at least a couple of hundred people on the call. Before the webinar started, the businessman in me began to get really intrigued, because as a businessman and a salesman, I was thinking, "200-plus prospects on the call . . . Two calls every week . . . $10,000 fee collected from each sale (that was the price that they charged for each movie) . . . With just a 1 percent closing ratio, that's over $2,000,000 in revenue every year." I ended up purchasing one of the overpriced movies just so I could see what they were doing in their selling process. I received a great return on investment (ROI) from the purchase, even though we never really used the movie. (By the way, once I went through the process, I figured out how to do this same process using contractors for less than $350 per movie, and I now teach it in The Leader's Institute Entrepreneur Boot Camp, which we offer to small-business owners about once per month in cities all over the United States.)

One great benefit of webinars and teleseminars is that you can easily record the sessions and offer them on demand from your website or from movie-sharing websites such as YouTube or even Facebook or LinkedIn. You can also have regular weekly seminars that you can use as free promotion, or you can charge a monthly fee to people who attend for an additional revenue stream. For instance, if you are financial planner, you might give weekly stock tips or tell your listeners about upcoming initial public offerings (IPOs). If you are a gym owner or manager, you might give weekly weight-loss tips or create a peer support group where members coach each other.

ASSOCIATION MEETINGS

It doesn't really matter what industry you are in. You have one or more trade associations available that you could be a member of if you like. For instance, there is a National Association of Pet Sitters for people who watch other people's pets in their own homes. To find your own trade association, just google "[your industry] trade association," and you'll likely find a few options. Some industry associations are very big and powerful, whereas others are fairly small. So your ability to speak to or in front of your chosen trade association will likely depend on the size and influence of the specific association.

For instance, a year or so after I started The Leader's Institute, I began to make myself available for local association meetings as a keynote speaker. I contacted the Dallas American Society for Trainers and Developers (ASTD) and learned that the waiting list to speak there was a couple of years long. Later on, I contacted the Fort Worth ASTD location, and they invited me to speak within two months. Only about 20 members attended the meeting, but one of those members was the human resources manager for the city of Fort Worth. She ended up sending a couple of people to my leadership classes every couple of months for the next two years. In the second year, she hired me to conduct a custom training session for her employees as well. That one free speech I gave ended up generating about $30,000 in income over the next two years.

One of my good friends designs and sells ventilation systems for restaurants, and he'd generate an entire year's worth of customers by speaking to the restaurant association once a year about the updated state laws and how to best service their ventilation systems.

If you tend to market to a specific trade, become a member of their association, or at the very least, offer to speak at the trade association monthly meetings or write articles for the trade association newsletter (more on that in my book *Cultivating Customers*). Sometimes you might have to sponsor the event in order to get an opportunity to speak, but even if you have to pay the association for the opportunity, when you speak at these events, it is as though the association is endorsing you as the expert.

In some associations, you will be speaking before and only to your competitors, but that is a great opportunity as well. You can now use the newsletter write-up or agenda for the event as a way to prove that you are the expert. You were the one who the association chose to speak, not the other 500 members! So, obviously, you are the expert according to the association. Whether or not the people in the audience will ever become your customers is irrelevant; the mere fact that you spoke in front of this group proves that you are an expert. The real secret to this is knowing that associations that have monthly meetings generally have at least one person who is responsible for finding a new speaker every single month, which is no small feat. Make yourself available, and eventually, you'll get an invitation to speak.

TRADE SHOWS

Perhaps one of the most lucrative places to speak is at industry trade shows. Trade shows have a high concentration of potential customers in one place, so if you can speak there, you are likely to gain a following. I remember the first trade show I attended. Since I was brand new and had absolutely zero credibility, the folks organizing the trade show weren't about to put me on their schedule, so I bought two trade show booth spaces that butted up to each other, and I picked spaces on the end of the row, where I knew there'd be a lot of traffic. When I set my area up, I put my booth in one booth section and put a flip chart and chairs in the other area facing my booth. I went to a sign store and purchased a sign that had a list of workshop topics and times, and I set the sign-up sheet on a tripod. I handed out a printed schedule to everyone who came by the booth. And every hour on

the half hour, I held a short informational seminar. Some of the topics had only one or two people sitting in the seats when I began, but almost all the seats would be filled by the time I ended. It was actually really fun, and many of the attendees hung around my booth at the end of each seminar.

Many trade shows will also have a schedule of breakout sessions. It takes more planning to get on the agenda for one of these sessions, but it can be well worth it. Most often, attendees will have a number of options to choose from, so the ones who come to your sessions will be interested in your topic.

MARKETING SEMINARS BY RESERVATION

Although teleseminars and webinars are less risky and less costly to conduct, some industries will likely require face-to-face meetings before customers will buy from you. For instance, financial planners often use free seminars that prospective customers can attend. This is key because people who hire financial planners have to be able to

trust their financial planner. It is easier to build that trust face-to-face and with a handshake. In cases such as this, in-person meetings will often work much better. The advantage of a marketing seminar versus a standard sales call or even a teleseminar is that you get the undivided attention of the audience for a longer period of time, and you can leverage your time and attract more customers in a shorter time period.

If you go to a businessperson's office for a sales call, he or she will likely give you only 15 to 45 minutes of time, but if someone takes the time to come to a seminar, you'll likely be able to communicate with that person uninterrupted for up to 2 hours. If you do a good job in the presentation, you can also use positive peer pressure from other audience members to persuade more skeptical potential customers to consider your services.

A couple of cautionary notes, though. When you give something away for free, people rarely value it. If you offer free seminars, this often translates into a *ton* of no-shows. If you need 100 people to attend, take reservations for 250 people and 100 might show up. If you need 50 people, take reservations for 125 people.

If you don't take reservations, no one will show up. I found that out the hard way. I had been teaching leadership training for about eight years, and I had a pretty decent client list. I started to notice that when participants would come through my leadership class, they would often tell me that the reason they were attending was to reduce their fear of public speaking. So I had this great idea to offer a free seminar about how to reduce public speaking fear as a lead-in to get people interested in attending my leadership class. I spoke quite often at chambers of commerce, business breakfasts, lead generation groups, and anywhere else that someone would let me, so I used these speeches as the promotion tool for the free seminar. I figured that if I gave something away that many people had already paid me thousands of dollars to receive, that I'd have hundreds of people in attendance. I spoke in front of about 2,500 people the month prior to the free seminar, and I promoted this free seminar every time I spoke. I received no fewer than 50 verbal RSVPs from audience members of these promotional presentations. I knew some wouldn't show up, but with that many confirmations, I was pretty confident that I was attracting a good-sized crowd.

I rented out a hotel meeting room the evening of the seminar, and I waited for all of the people to show up. We started at 6:30 PM, and at 6:29 PM, the first person showed up. At 6:35 PM, she was still the only other person there. At 6:40 PM, she was *still* the only person there. And at 6:45 PM, I went over to her and told her that I was going to have to cancel the seminar, and I told her that I'd give her a big discount if she wanted to come take my leadership class. She didn't, by the way. It was really embarrassing.

I learned a couple of important lessons, though. Now, I always take reservations for any free seminar, and I, or someone from my office, also make a phone call to every attendee prior to the meeting. That way, I always have a better idea of how many people will really show up. I've also found that if I give away something to people just for coming, attendance is much better. For instance, I might give away a Kindle version of one of my books. The Kindle version of the book is just a digital file, so it costs me nothing to give one away. Or sometimes I tell attendees that I'll be available to autograph a copy of one of my books, and then, of course, I sell them the book when they attend the meeting.

Since that first big mistake, I have had a lot better success with promotional seminars, and I've also come across other companies that use this technique pretty well.

For instance, I once was invited to a seminar at the Bentley car dealership in Dallas. The hook was that the dealership was going to provide a three-course lunch for attendees, and each of us would get a chance to test-drive a new Bentley. I was busy, and I figured this was just a high-priced sales pitch—but it still sounded pretty cool. I moved my schedule around and accepted the invitation. They hired an executive chef to cater the event, and the food was impeccable. One of the corporate spokesmen opened the meeting and presented a short slide show about the history of the Bentley company and how much success the company has had in racing and performance cars. And the event ended with a test-drive for each of us. It was a very well-organized event. I started a conversation with the sales manager of the dealership and asked him, "Just out of curiosity, how many people who come to this event actually end up buying a Bentley?" He told me that more than 25 percent of the attendees end up buying a car from them within the next year. Then I asked him what percentage of walk-in prospects ended up buying, and he told me less than 5 percent. So the dealership had a strategy that helped them increase their closing ratio fivefold by using a targeted marketing seminar. (Just as an FYI, although this was a very pricey experiment for the company, it really paid off, because the company had to generate only one sale from every six events to break even. Bentleys are really, really expensive!)

Regardless of what you decide to give away, it's usually a good idea to give an incentive for attendees to show up. Personally, I think that the best incentive to make sure that attendees show up to your meeting is to charge a fee.

PAID PUBLIC SEMINARS

Seminars that individuals can attend for a fee can be a fantastic way to promote yourself or your company, because you will also receive income for the time that you spend organizing and conducting the event. Remember that your time is valuable, and you should be very careful about giving it away for free. In addition, when attendees pay a fee to attend an event, they are much more committed to show up. People are busy, so if we let them attend for free and something else comes up, they will think, "We'll, I'm not losing anything if I don't go, so why don't I just wait for the next one?" If there is a fee to be lost, though, they will have to determine which is more valuable: the new thing that popped up or the fee that's going to be lost. The bigger the fee, the bigger the commitment will be.

If you happen to be in an industry that already conducts seminars, such as education, financial planning, investing, and the like, then charging people to attend your seminars is pretty easy. If you are in an industry where seminars are not common, though, you might have to get creative. For instance, if you are a family dentist, you might conduct a teeth-whitening seminar where you teach attendees which teeth-whitening products are a scam and how to keep your teeth white between dental visits. If you manage a restaurant, you might host a cooking seminar about how to get your family to sit down to dinner. If you are a psychologist, you might offer a seminar on reducing stress without medication.

The fee that you charge is pretty important. The relationship between the number of attendees and the fee that you charge is a bell curve. If you charge too little, you look cheap and potential attendees won't value the service. If you charge too much, most potential attendees won't even consider attending the event. I wish I could tell you what fee would be best for you, but every industry is different. I'll use my own industry as an example so that you can see how the pricing creates a perception of the product. In adult education seminars, if the fee is $0 to $100, the perception will be that the event is going to be a sales pitch for something that has a much higher price—or that the seminar is simply not good enough to charge a higher fee. If I were to offer a seminar for this fee, I'd likely attract only young people, people who are just starting their careers, or those who are transitioning to a new career. A fee of $100 to $400 will give the perception that real teaching will occur, but the prospective attendees will likely expect the speaker to try to sell them a bunch of books or tapes at the conclusion. A fee of $400 to $1,000 will ensure attendees that they will receive quality instruction without anyone trying to strong-arm them into buying more during the seminar. And a fee of over $1,000 will give the perception that the seminar is for fairly high-level executives or an elite group.

If the dentist conducting the teeth-whitening seminar charges $100, though, the perception will be that the attendees will get some type of result from the seminar, because teeth-whitening kits are typically less than $50. If the restaurant manager charges $75 for the cooking seminar, then that might instill that the seminar is a quality seminar because a nice meal at a restaurant is usually less than $50. On the other hand, if you are a financial planner and offer a seminar on day trading and charge $75 or $100, then you are not likely to get a great showing. Charge $5,000, though, and you might have to have a waiting list.

When you set the fee, make sure (1) that you generate enough revenue to make the activity worth your while and (2) that when people walk away from the seminar, they are sure that the benefit they received significantly outweighed the fee that they paid.

PAID CONSULTING MEETINGS

Paid consulting meetings can be for one person or large groups, and they can be a great way to build a following of loyal customers. The meetings can be in person, on the phone, or even online (webinars). They can be free, or they can be used as a revenue stream. Most people I know who use this venue well use it as a follow-up to a purchase or an add-on purchase for something else. For instance, if your company provides software to large companies, then a good add-on to the software sale would be webinar consulting sessions after the purchase.

When people attend our Fearless Presentations classes, the instructors offer two phone consulting sessions after the class as a part

of the tuition. It helps the participants better implement the techniques that we teach in the seminar, and as a result, they end up raving about the program. In addition, this simple follow-up technique fans the flame, making these participants more likely to tell others about the class that they attended. Once these participants complete the two free sessions, if they want to continue with an additional session, they can for a small fee.

Attorneys and accountants will often offer a free introductory consulting session as a way to generate, and sometimes screen, new clients. These same professionals can offer follow-up sessions for a fee as well and generate more income and more satisfied customers.

A realtor can do consulting with investors on buying and selling property, short sells, or foreclosures. Bankers can do consulting on small-business loans. An air-conditioning mechanic can do consulting on making your home more energy efficient. A landscaper can do consulting sessions on which plants do best in that specific region. Remember, what is common knowledge to you is uncommon to others, so people will pay you for your expertise.

RADIO AND TV SHOWS

Every major city in America and many suburbs and smaller cities have AM and FM talk radio stations and dozens of talk shows every week. Although the weekday prime-time shows are typically syndicated national shows and difficult to be invited on as a guest, in the evenings and weekends, the hosts and producers are much more willing to bring guests on to inform their audiences about something important to them. Many of the weekend shows are actually segments that are purchased by amateur talk show host or hosts-of-the-future who buy the time from the radio station and then sell their own advertising to fund the show. Many of these advertisers are actually the "guests" on the show, so the host will likely promote the guest very well during

the segment. The downside of these types of programs is that they are often not very entertaining and will often sound like a self-serving sales pitch, so they won't have a big audience.

However, real entertainment shows or topical shows are plentiful on talk radio. I once was invited to be a guest on a noontime show on Urban Radio in Washington, DC. The host had come across one of my articles about public speaking, and she wanted to do a segment on how minorities could use public speaking to build their success. It was a fun and easy interview, and she even had a few callers at the end of the interview who asked me questions. I had an absolute blast, and it was great public relations for me.

That particular interview was an absolute accident, though. If the host had not read my article, she would have never known about me and I would have never known about her or her show. So, for the most part, you'll just have to spend some time doing some research for shows that will be a good fit. The best way to find a show to contact is to google "talk radio [your industry]." Once you find a show that might be a good fit, look on that show's website to find out who the producer is. The producer's name and e-mail address or contact information will often be easy to find, because this is how they get potential guests. If you can't find the producer's contact information, call the radio station and ask for it. Most often, the station will freely give it to you. Then send a short e-mail to the producer with a one-paragraph segment idea along with why you are the expert. Wait a day or so, and then follow up with a phone call as well.

One of the fabulous technology improvements that has occurred over the past five years is the advent of Internet radio. One of the advantages of Internet radio is that if you want to be a guest on a program, there are thousands of programs to choose from. And if you aren't satisfied with just being a guest, then you can create your own show. Most laptops now have audio and video recorders, and you can record an episode of a radio program using online programs or even your computer's movie program. Save the recording as either a movie file, an audio file, or even a text file, and upload the file to a podcast distribution system. Don't let the word *podcast* confuse you if you are new to this technology. It is just a computer word for a recorded audio or video program on the Internet.

The most popular podcast system is on Apple's iTunes, but there are literally hundreds (if not thousands) of podcast-sharing websites. With regular broadcast radio, when you appear on a program for 15 minutes, only the people who are actually listening to that particular show on that particular radio station will ever hear you. Once the segment ends, your appearance is lost in space. However, with podcasts, since the segment is recorded and each episode is listed on demand, people who want to hear the segment can listen to it at any time and it is available forever. You can also send links to your interview segment to prospective customers. Remember the old jukeboxes where you put a coin in and chose whatever song you wanted to hear and the machine would play it? Before jukeboxes, you either had to wait by the radio all day to hear the song that you wanted, or you had to pony up and go buy the record. Podcasts are like a *huge* jukebox with an unlimited number of selections, and anyone with an Internet connection has access.

In addition to the radio and podcasts, television will also give you a big audience. The process is similar to the process for radio but realize that achieving a guest spot on a television show is much more challenging. I would suggest that you hire a professional TV coach and invest in a good public relations firm before attempting to try to get a TV spot. Unlike radio, where many of the programs are designed to educate the listening audience, television is more geared toward controversy. So, if you are able to get one of these spots on television, there is a good chance that the interviewer will be purposefully trying to trip you up or embarrass you. Be extremely careful.

JOINT VENTURE SEMINARS

Joint venture seminars can be the "mother lode" for new business relationships and new revenue streams. To go this route, you find one or more entrepreneurs or salespeople who are not in direct

competition with you and who have a list of clients or customers. Then promote a joint seminar to both your list of prospects and customers and their lists of prospects and customers. The easiest way to do this is with a teleconference where one of the joint venture partners interviews the other, but you can also promote an in-person seminar as well. Remember, though, in this process, you have to give to get, so the bigger your client list or prospect list is, the better joint venture partners you will attract.

For instance, a furniture store can partner with an interior designer to promote a seminar on staging the furniture in model homes for home-building companies. Both of these companies could even provide the seminar for free and ask that their literature be offered to new home buyers. The interior designer would call all of his or her clients who are model home stagers, as would the manager of the furniture store. Since both of their lists would be fairly small, neither of these folks by themselves would likely be able to attract enough attendees to make the seminar worthwhile, but both lists together would have a much better chance for success.

A fitness coach at a gym could contact the manager of the local organic food restaurant, and the two of them could organize a weight-loss seminar. The fitness coach could promote the seminar to current and past clients, and the restaurant manager can hand out brochures to everyone who buys a meal from his or her restaurant for a couple of weeks.

Successful Internet marketers use this venue to attract new customers with great success. In fact, Internet marketers with big lists of customers and potential customers will often use this venue only as a way to bring in new customers. For instance, say an Internet marketing company gives away a free newsletter for a couple of years and gains 20,000 subscribers who have opted in to their e-mail list. These Internet marketers will then often go in on a joint venture with noncompetitive companies to market additional products and services to these 20,000 subscribers in exchange for partner number two promoting partner number one's products and service to their big list as well. (By the way, if you are interested in learning how to create a list of tens of thousands of potential clients, make sure and pick up a copy of my book *Cultivating Customers*.)

Most Internet marketers will tell you that for every 10,000 names and e-mail addresses that you get on your contact list, you'll be able to generate about $1,000,000 worth of income every year. Joint ventures are a good way to allow your list of clients and prospects to generate income for you and your company.

CHAPTER 7

How to Make Millions of Dollars Using Presentation Skills on YouTube and Podcasting Websites

"Counsel woven into the fabric of real life is wisdom."
—Walter Benjamin

Okay, so you've designed a great presentation with five really important and well-vetted bullet points, and you've practiced delivering the presentation a couple of times to ensure you have a killer delivery. Once you deliver the presentation for the intended audience, though, the value of the presentation is over. Wouldn't it be great if you could share this information with thousands of audiences versus a single audience, build your credibility immensely, and add a new revenue stream that becomes what wealthy people used to call "mailbox money," where the revenue comes every week or month without you ever doing anything else? Enter YouTube!

You will always practice your presentation at least once or twice before you deliver the presentation to your actual audience, so during one of these practice sessions, why not just set up a video

recorder? Remember that this wisdom that you are sharing, although pretty common knowledge to you, is something that people outside of your industry know very little about. It is information that is valuable.

You can record high-quality videos using your laptop or even with your smartphone now, but if you want to pay a professional to record you instead, the fees are fairly small now and well worth it.

Once you start to think differently about being an expert in an industry and using technology to capitalize on that expertise, you will start to see opportunities everywhere. For instance, a few years ago, my wife and I bought a new house, and for the first time in my life I was a pool owner. I'm a pretty good swimmer and I was a lifeguard in college, but I've never actually maintained a pool. A few days before we moved into the house, the man we bought the house from took me step-by-step through the whole process of how to check the chemical levels, how the valves worked, how to clean the filter, and how to backwash the filter. He also gave me all of the percentages and numbers to look at to know when to do all of these things. I was feeling pretty confident; after all, I'm a smart guy, and I have a pretty good memory. A week or so later, after we had moved in, I went back out to the pool. Unfortunately, everything was a little fuzzier than I expected. The pipes looked like a maze, and there were all kinds of valves and switches. I couldn't remember the numbers, and I had to go out and reidentify each of the valves by trial and error. I took a lot of trips down to the pool store, and the guy at the counter could see that I was in over my head. He looked at me and said, "You know that we have a pool school, right?" Turns out, the pool company will send a tech out to my house for less than $100 and have the tech take me through the entire system. He suggested that I record the guy when he came out.

It was brilliant. I knew that if I just had the pool technician come out and walk me through it one more time, I might be fuzzy on the details at the conclusion of this coaching, too. But if I had a recording, I could review it after the technician left. By the way, it worked perfectly. The technician let me record him, and he walked me through the whole process step-by-step. The pool school got me through the normal day-to-day maintenance of the pool, but at the end of summer, I had to clean the filter by myself for the first time. Since it was something new to me, I pulled out my smartphone and forwarded the video that I recorded to the part where the technician cleaned the filter. Then all I had to do was follow along.

This is exactly the type of information or expertise that is valuable to potential customers and that can funnel new customers to your website. The pool supply company could either give this information away for free in order to attract new customers, or they could sell the online pool school for a lower price and increase profit.

GIVE INFORMATION AWAY TO ATTRACT A FUNNEL OF NEW CUSTOMERS

My friend Mike Koenigs is the cofounder of a company called Traffic Geyser (www.tli-trafficgeyser.com), which is a website where members can upload a single video and have the video added to dozens (and sometimes hundreds) of different video-sharing websites. His philosophy is to create 10 different videos with your top 10 most frequently asked questions from customers and clients and upload those videos to video-sharing sites to funnel customers to your website.

Using the pool supply company as the example, the owner of the pool supply company could break up the recording of the pool school into five to ten 2-minute videos on each of the topics covered in the school. For instance, one video might be about how to connect the vacuum cleaner hose to the skimmers to manually clean the pool. Another might be about how to regularly clean the skimmers themselves. One might be about how to keep the chemicals in balance. One might be about how to maintain the heater in cold weather. One might be about how to backwash and clean the filter. If the pool supply company gave these videos away for free, they could have each of the individual videos feed back to a single page of their website to access all of the videos in one place and just require that the viewers enter their e-mail address to access them. Every time a new person enters an e-mail address, the pool company's list of potential customers grows. They can send out e-mails to this list with coupons for pool supplies or maintenance service.

"Oh, but what if the pool company is just a local store?" There is almost no such thing as a local store anymore. For instance, the pool company could simply put the phrase, "Order today, and we'll deliver it tomorrow" all over their website. FedEx makes any local company a big player in the world market.

So what does it cost to give this information away? Well, by giving the pool school away for free, the company is losing the potential to make a one-time $79 fee a few times per month from new local pool owners. I mean, really, how many first-time pool owners are created in a single neighborhood each year? However, when you think about the number of first-time pool owners in the world each year, the market is incredibly bigger. The company has the potential to create new customers every day via mail order. In fact, the company could create a membership where customers get all of their pool chemicals shipped out every month and delivered by UPS or FedEx, with the monthly fee automatically charged to a credit card.

CHARGE A FEE FOR YOUR EXPERTISE

Another option is to charge a fee on the front end for the information. Instead of using the individual videos as marketing pieces to funnel leads to your website, make them an online study course. When the pool supply company sends a technician out to conduct the pool school, the company has to pay the technician to do it. Let's say that the technician gets paid $50 to conduct the training, so the company keeps only $29 of the $79. If the pool supply company supplied the videos online and purchasers could access each video on an as-needed basis, the company could charge a onetime fee of $39 or $49 and actually make a little more profit than what they were making when they were charging more. In addition, to make the purchase, the buyer would need to enter his or her name, mailing address, and e-mail address, so the company now knows of a potential new purchaser of pool supplies as well.

Once the videos are created, they can be copied over to a DVD or a flash drive. That way, if the company decided to continue to do the in-person pool schools, they can charge an extra fee to give the videos to the customer as follow-up materials after the technician leaves. Added value and added service lead to more loyal customers.

Regardless of whether you use videos as a marketing tool to let the world know about your expertise or if you use videos as a new revenue stream, it is a good idea to keep a record of the presentations that you have created and delivered in the past. A video recording is an easy way to keep track of these past presentations.

USE A PODCAST TO GENERATE NEW CUSTOMERS AND REVENUE

Recall from Chapter 6 that the word *podcast* is just a geeky word for Internet broadcast or audio or video recording on the Internet. Using podcast websites, you can create a channel that is basically your own personal radio station that plays the content you create and upload. The podcast could be as simple as the few videos that the pool supply company made, or it could be a daily teleseminar or webinar, with new content added every day.

I have a friend who started conducting an in-home Bible study group at his house while he was attending a seminary in Dallas.

He wanted to do really in-depth studies, because he realized that it was difficult for people to learn the content from the Bible in the standard 15- to 40-minute sermons that they tend to get in a normal church service. Within the first year, though, he noticed a big problem. Because the study was so comprehensive, when new people started to attend the sessions, they became frustrated pretty quickly because they were so far behind.

A few years ago, he changed the format to a webinar series versus an in-person series, and all of the sudden, his number of attendees jumped and grew exponentially. He still has dozens of people who attend the sessions live every Wednesday night, but now, his attendees can access the webinar anytime they want. At the conclusion of each webinar, everyone who has ever attended any of the sessions receives an e-mail with a link to the most current recording. If someone misses a few weeks, that person can access the archives and catch up. And when new people join the study, they have the choice of jumping into the live series, starting at the beginning of the current series, or even starting over from scratch with the very first recording. Each participant can go through the sessions on his or her own schedule, so if anyone wants to listen to two or three sessions each week, he or she can.

Of course, the pastor doesn't charge his attendees to view or listen to his recordings, but if you use the same type of strategy for your company, you certainly can. You can either charge viewers for every session that they watch, or you can create a membership where a monthly fee is assessed regardless of how many sessions are viewed.

Another great way to create a podcast is to hold weekly tele-seminars where participants can come with questions for the expert or where you interview other experts in your industry. Every time you add new content that will be beneficial to your customers or prospects, you can send them an announcement e-mail; if you have a podcast channel, those e-mails go out automatically, helping keep you and your company top of mind for these customers.

CHAPTER 8

If You Want Big Contracts, Get Really Good at Short List Presentations

"Timid salesmen have skinny kids."

—Zig Ziglar

In many industries, prospective buyers will request proposals from a few vendors, weed through those proposals, narrow down the possible vendors to a short list, and then have each of the short list vendors participate in an interview or a formal presentation to determine which company wins the contract. Keep in mind that these purchasers don't always use the presentation as the determining factor in choosing their vendor, but it will at least be a factor in excluding vendors if nothing else. However, if you are a qualified vendor, you give the best presentation, and no other political factors are involved, you have a good shot at closing the contract.

The main thing to remember about these interviews is that the purchasers (usually a committee of some kind) will make the assumption that you are a qualified vendor simply because you have been invited to present and compete for the contract. The committees often have a team of people who weed through the thick proposals to exclude any companies that aren't qualified. So unless you prove otherwise to them, they will almost always automatically assume that you are qualified.

In Chapter 1, I stated:

The confidence that a person shows when standing up to speak is often perceived by others to be competence in what he or she does.

This statement is vitally true in short list presentations and interviews. When a presenter participates in an interview, the committee will determine that person's competence based on the content delivered and the confidence that the presenter exhibits when delivering this content. The presenter can be the most experienced, the most seasoned, the most qualified, and the most recognized expert in the entire industry, but if the person looks timid or nervous or in any way sounds unsure or confused, then that presenter will often be excluded from consideration immediately (especially if other, less qualified presenters look confident and sure of themselves). The good news is that if you are one of the less qualified presenters but you look extremely confident and sure of yourself, then there is a good chance that the committee might pass over these other presenters and consider you.

All other things considered, confidence and surety in the presentation mean more than actual experience or expertise during the interview process. Remember, this is true only because the people making the decision assume that all of the presenters are qualified; otherwise, they wouldn't have been invited to present.

DIG YOUR WELL BEFORE YOU ARE THIRSTY

Since self-confidence is so important in these types of presentations, don't wait until two days before the presentation to start preparing for it. By the way, I'm not talking about the presentation itself. I'm referring to the preparing of presenters well in advance so that when the opportunity presents itself, you and your presenters are able to capitalize on that opportunity.

About six years ago, I was brought in as a speaking coach for a joint venture between a big engineering firm and a minority general contracting company. The companies were trying to close a commercial town square retail center, so the stakes were very high. The prospective client wanted to meet the team that they would be working with, so the presentation team was composed of the general contractor, one of the vice presidents of the engineering form, the project manager, the superintendent, the lead engineer, and a couple of other team members who would appear but not have speaking parts. The general contractor, vice president, and project manager had all participated in countless presentations and were very seasoned. The superintendent had much less experience as a presenter; he was much more comfortable with power tools than a slide show. However, he was prepared and ready to do his part. The lead engineer, though, had never in his career participated in any type of sales presentation and had likely given only a small number of any other type of presentation as well. He was totally unprepared to have a contract worth hundreds of millions of dollars weighing on his shoulders.

Luckily, we were able to minimize his part in the presentation and build his confidence so that he performed adequately, but every single person on the team (even the engineer) knew that he was the weakest link on the team. When the presentation was finished,

I went to the vice president of the engineering firm and mentioned to him that he put an enormous amount of pressure onto the shoulders of a man who was totally unprepared. If that contract had fallen through as a result of the presentation they just completed, he'd have himself to blame, not the engineer. This particular engineer had been working for the company for more than 10 years and had never been trained for a vital part of his success.

Over the next two years, we conducted presentation training for every single person in the company. By the way, once we had trained all of the executives and then trained the next generation of leaders, I figured that my role as their presentation trainer would end. I was wrong. The vice president had already seen so much value from the earlier classes that he ended up having me do additional classes for everyone else in the office, including the receptionist. Over these two years, his team closed more than 80 percent of their short list presentations (an incredibly high percentage). After the first few successes, we started to realize something very simple but profound. Almost every one of the competitors for these projects went into the presentation with at least one or two really good presenters, but they were always accompanied by a supporting cast who were hit or miss in terms of portraying confidence when they stood up to speak. Our teams were always polished and in control—right down to the people sitting at the back of the room who weren't even involved in the presentation but who, at times, answered questions from the committee when needed. It made a big difference.

About a year after I taught the last class for this company, the largest general contracting company in the United States made an offer to buy out the company. Almost every team member who went through the coaching ended up with hundreds of thousands of dollars in stock options in the purchasing company, and the high-level executives generated millions in stock in the bigger company. Everybody won. The clients got better service, the engineering firm got tremendous growth and created hundreds of new jobs, the executives created a massive amount of wealth, and the employees experienced an increase in their standard of living.

Don't wait until a big company invites you to compete for a big contract before you prepare yourself and your team to be able to capitalize on the opportunity.

Dig your well before you are thirsty.

SHOW CLIENTS HOW YOU CAN HELP THEM GET WHAT THEY REALLY WANT

We covered this quite a bit in Chapter 2 on how to design your presentations, but it is so important to success in sales presentations for you to focus on what the customer wants, not what you want to say. To do this, you will need to do some research ahead of time. If nothing else, google your potential client. You'd be amazed what you can find out.

One of the most fun classes that I have ever taught was a couple of years ago when I was hired to do sales training for a brewery in Salt Lake City. (They had a bar downstairs where they held tastings of the fresh beer right as it was brewed!) One of the sessions I covered in the class was about how to do research and how important that research can be in helping the company better understand and persuade clients. I spent an hour or so prior to class searching for information about the brewery and each of the individuals attending the class. In that hour, I uncovered who the executives of the company were and found a lot of information about their backgrounds. I found an article about the sales manager who hired me in which he was being interviewed because he was a car collector. I found out where one of the ladies in class grew up, what college she went to, what sorority she was a member of, the names of a few of her best friends, and what companies her best friends work for. I found out that one of the other sales reps started out working in the family art business and that he was named after his uncle who owns that art business. (The amount of information that I found in such a short period of time was actually kind of creepy, but shockingly effective.)

When researching the company, I learned that it is the only brewery in the country whose energy needs are being provided entirely through renewable forms of energy. This sounded like a great selling point, so I did some more research. It turns out that the company paid the same fee to the electric company as every one of its competitors, but because of its environmental philosophy, the brewery was purchasing offsets that were used to generate an equal amount of green energy, such as wind and solar. This meant that the brewery's expenses were higher than its competitors'. Without knowing anything about the company's prices or pricing structure, within an hour, I was able to find out that, most likely, its prices were higher than the competitors' or its profit margin was going to be thinner. If the profit margin was lower, then the company would likely have to sacrifice somewhere else, either lower sales commissions or maybe less marketing. I wasn't exactly sure at the time which of these was the case, but the research allowed me to ask much better questions. The answers to those questions helped me provide a better course for the company.

You want to do the same type of thing when you begin to research your clients before these interviews. If you are going to be presenting to a school board, go to its website and read up on the members. Most public hearings such as school board meetings are taped and offered on demand on the school district's website. You can watch some of these recordings and get a better feel for each individual member and what that person deems most important. You can do a news search for all the members on the committee and see if any news stories have been written about them. Look to see if they have a LinkedIn account or even a Facebook page. Try to collect as much information as you can about the company and the individuals making the purchasing decision.

Once you do some preliminary research, you will want to design some questions to ask the client that will help you uncover what the real needs and wants of the client are. For some reason, most presenters skip this step all together. During one of these short list coaching sessions, I suggested that the group of presenters call the contact person who was organizing the presentation schedule to help us clarify what was most important to the committee, and one of the presenters paused, looked at me, and said, "But it is a sealed bid situation." I wasn't sure exactly what difference that made, so I just paused and didn't say anything. He continued with, "Since it is a sealed bid, we can't really talk to anyone before they open up the bids."

"Who said that was a rule?" I asked.

The silence was my answer. They all assumed that they couldn't call the organizer, but they went back and checked the request for quote (RFQ) and found that there was actually a phone number listed within the text of the RFQ for just such a call. Within a few minutes, they found out that although the overall price was important, the organization had set a pretty aggressive schedule that was actually much more important to the success of the project than the price—and the organizer freely volunteered this information. We altered the presentation dramatically as a result.

Once you figure out what is important to the purchasers, design your presentation focused on the three most important points.

I like to use buying a car as an example to explain this process, because it is often so obvious once you see the process happen in real life. Whenever someone purchases a car, the person will have a hierarchy of car features based on what is most important to him or her. Let's say that the car buyer travels a lot by car for work and often drives 3 to 4 hours a few times per week to travel from city to city. He uses the mileage for the car as a tax deduction. The car that the buyer owns now has been a great car, but it has been in the shop twice this year, so the buyer has spent money on repairs and rental cars. He also has sales samples to carry in the car when he travels for business and a wife and two kids when he is at home, so passenger space and cargo room are both pretty important.

So the buyer's hierarchy is as follows:

Dependability + Warranty + Gas Mileage + Cargo Space + Passenger Room + Price

The buyer walks into a car dealership and the salesperson asks, "So what kind of car are you looking for?"

If the buyer has done a little research, he might give a name of a model. But let's say that the buyer says something like, "Maybe a minivan or an SUV."

The salesperson takes him to the lot and picks one minivan and one SUV, and they go on a test-drive in each. At the end of the test-drive, the salesperson asks, "Which did you like better?" The buyer selects the SUV.

This happens in a very similar way on two additional car lots, but because none of the salespeople asked even a few preliminary questions about what the purchaser wanted, the only real information that the buyer has to make a decision is the test-drive itself, the gas mileage sticker on the window, and the price. Mentally, the buyer will go through the checklist either consciously or subconsciously.

Dependability? Well, all three salespeople said that their brand was the most dependable, so at least two of them were lying. Warranty? Well, each of them had a three-year warranty, but I'm not sure which company best backs their warranty. Gas mileage? The sticker said that the SUV from the second company had the best number, but they were all within one point of each other. Cargo space? SUV number one looked biggest, but they were all pretty similar. Passenger room? SUV number three had third-row seats, but it cost $2,000 more than the other two.

Since none of the salespeople took an interest in the customer, he makes the purchasing decision based on the numbers in the window (either the mileage or the price). In fact, the buyer might actually choose to pay $2,000 more for the SUV that has the third-row seat—the *fifth* most important aspect. However, it didn't have to be that way. All it would have taken was a single salesperson to ask a couple of questions. If any one of the salespeople had determined that dependability and warranty were most important, then the salesperson could have introduced the buyer to the service manager and asked the service manager about the dependability of the car. That little extra contact would probably be enough to put that particular car over the top, because the other salespeople did so little.

I find that short list presentations and interviews are often organized this way. Presenters often spend a lot of time talking about themselves, their company, their experience, and their expertise, and they very rarely pause and focus on what the client really wants. If the presenters can prove to the client that their team can give them just one of the things that they really want, they will often get a nice response. If the presentation team can give the client two or three things that are wanted, the decision becomes a no-brainer.

"Since you are a road warrior, I know how important having access to your car is, so you don't want it to be in the shop. Just by buying a new car, any new car, you're going to eliminate that repair cost and inconvenience that you've been experiencing recently. Out of all of the SUVs that we sell, this particular model is the one that we see least of in the service department. In fact, I'll walk you through the service area as we head back to my office, and we can do a spot-check to see what cars are in there. This car has the standard three-year or 30,000-mile warranty, but since you drive 15,000 miles per year on average, I'm going to upgrade the warranty to include 45,000 miles so that it fits the way you drive. This car gets only 19 miles to the gallon in the city, which is the price that you pay for the passenger room and extra cargo space, but on the highway, that goes up to 23 miles to the gallon, so that will help you a little. This one is a little smaller than the ones that have the third-row seats, but the bigger versions lower your gas mileage by about 3 miles to the gallon. Since the IRS gives only you 50 cents per mile, every little bit helps, though. Do you have your samples with you? Let's go see how they fit in the cargo area?"

See how much better that presentation is than, "What kind of car are you looking at?" and "Which did you like better?"

Focus on what the client wants and needs, and you will help the client make a better, more informed decision!

SHOW THE COMMITTEE THAT YOU ARE A TEAM

Two of the main things that purchasers are looking for, since they already assume that you are qualified, is whether they like you and whether they can work with you. One often-overlooked aspect that will build great rapport with the audience is the way that the presenters edify and interact with one another. Are the presenters showing respect to their team members by building up the expertise of the other presenters, or is there only one main presenter who is building up himself or herself? If your group is the former, then the audience is much more likely to respect you and want to work with you.

One of the groups who I worked with in the past did this by inserting their introductions for one another into the heart of the presentation, versus giving a quick introduction for each presenter at the beginning of the presentation. The lead presenter covered the first point, gave an example, and included a cool analogy. Then he introduced the second presenter by saying, "I know that the schedule is vital to the success of this project, so I'd like to introduce David (first name only) to you. He'll be your project manager, and he has a phenomenal success rate at completing projects either on time or early. In fact, three of his last five projects were each completed at least two weeks prior to the contracted deadline. David?" When David introduced the engineer, he gave a similar introduction. Every time that they switched to a new presenter, the previous presenter would build up the credibility of the next speaker before he or she even said a word. It worked wonderfully.

USE SHOWMANSHIP TO MAKE YOU AND YOUR TEAM MEMORABLE

I've given a lot of examples of different types of showmanship you can use in your presentations, but keep in mind that everything I have given you in this book has already been used, so it may not be as fresh or impactful as something new that you make up yourself.

For example, I explained earlier in the book how one company used the big posters with the portraits of the team members as a way for the committee to remember them. The reason why we had to come up with that piece of showmanship was that in an earlier presentation, the same group had been using a place mat for the committee members. The place mat was pretty cool, and I thought it was a great idea. It was an 11 × 17 piece of glossy card stock that included the company name and logo, a portrait of each presenter with a short biography, the agenda bullet points, and even a space for notes. These place mats looked great, and they seemed to be very functional.

The committee meeting where the presentations were being made was open to the public, so I was able to sit in the gallery and watch the team that I was coaching, as well as all the other presentation teams, give their presentations. Just before the first team started presenting, they gave the committee a place mat. The second team gave the committee a place mat. Our team was third, and we gave them a place mat. The fourth team didn't provide a place mat, but they gave a terrible presentation and I got the feeling that this might have been the first sales presentation that the team had ever delivered. I suspect they were excluded pretty quickly.

The point is that somewhere along the way, some company had a great idea to give out a place mat, and because it was such a good idea, everyone started doing it. Once everyone started doing it, it was no longer showmanship. So our group decided to do something different, and the big posters worked really well. Guess what happened the next time they presented? Correct. A bunch of the other teams had big life-sized posters.

In another presentation, one of our competitors decided to make a huge schedule board that was about 4 feet tall and 10 feet wide, and the team used that board as the agenda for their presentation; they never used a single PowerPoint slide. It was a very well-organized presentation, and they delivered it beautifully. They ended up winning the contract.

The next time we competed with that company, we knew we had to be better. We created an animated video of the schedule, where the committee could see step-by-step what each phase of the project would look like.

When one company does something new and fresh, it gets noticed. When everybody does the same thing, though, you're likely to just get lost in the crowd. So be creative.

CHAPTER 9

Fearless Question and Answer Sessions

"Before I refuse to take your questions, I have an opening statement."
—Ronald Reagan

Many presenters are most fearful of the question and answer periods, because they feel like they can't really prepare for them. However, question and answer periods are not only fairly easy to prepare for but also a fantastic way to prove that you are the expert.

Before we cover how to conduct question and answer sessions, let's first talk about when question and answer sessions are helpful and when to avoid them. We'll also talk about two different types of questions you will be asked.

WHEN TO USE QUESTION AND ANSWER SESSIONS

If you are in control of the agenda and have the option of whether to include a question and answer session, don't put the session in. In real-life presentations, the last thing you want to do is have people hold all of their questions until the end of your presentation. If someone has a question about something that I am covering, I would much rather have the person ask me the question when it comes up versus having the person with the question being confused during most of my presentation and then asking the question at the end. It's a better policy to encourage questions throughout the presentation than finishing early and giving people a few minutes after the presentation to ask questions.

If, however, someone else is in control of the agenda, and a question and answer session at the end of the presentation is required, then make sure, before you receive the first question, that you understand the two different types of questions you will likely get asked.

Questions for Clarity

Most questions are being asked so that the person asking the question can gain some clarity. The person asking the question is confused or didn't understand something that you previously discussed. Sometimes, because of a short time period, we have to rush through information, and as a result, we will get a number of these types of questions. Interestingly enough, if you design your presentation using the most important point method and insert some stories and examples, you will rarely get questions like this.

If you do get these questions, answer them with a short answer (if the question lends itself to a short answer).

"When can your team get started?"

"Next week."

If the question is more in depth, treat it like a new key point and use an example, story, or some other type of impact idea to answer the question.

"You said that phase two would take between two weeks and six weeks. What could cause the variance, and how long are you expecting for this project?"

"Let me give you a couple of examples. Phase two could take as little as two weeks as it did in the . . ."

These types of questions are not being asked to test you or to throw you off your game. They are being asked only because the questioner wants some additional information. These questions are easy to answer, and you should feel good about your answer when you give it to the questioner.

Questions to Test the Presenter

The second type of question is more challenging, because these questions are designed to test the presenter. Often these questions are asked with an unmistakable tone. At times, the person who is asking the question either has an agenda or may just be a jerk trying to embarrass the speaker. However, more often, especially in interviews, the questioner has a set of prepared questions that he or she is asking every presenter and will then compare how each presenter or team answered the questions. Regardless of why the person is asking the question, though, the presenter will need to answer the question with tact and control.

For these types of questions, answer them very quickly, but clarify your answer with an example or a story immediately. Here is an example:

"When was the last time you missed a schedule deadline, and why did it happen?"

"Last winter, we were working on a project in Minneapolis, and toward the latter stages of the project, a winter storm hit the area, shutting down most transportation near the project for the better part of a week. Unfortunately, that started a chain reaction, because some subcontractors had to be scheduled weeks in advance, and they couldn't do their part of the project until earlier contractors were finished. Dave was our project manager on that project, too, and he got word from one of the subcontractors that if we couldn't get this subcontracting team in within 14 days, that they wouldn't be able to return for more than 30 days. So Dave pulled a lot of strings and had one of the earlier subcontractors pull in a second crew at our expense so that we didn't miss that critical deadline. Even though we missed over a week because of weather, the project still completed within four days of the scheduled end date. So that is exactly the reason why you want Dave and his team on your project. Things are not always going to go as planned; you need someone on your team who is going to go the extra mile to minimize damage and increase your success when something outside of any of our control occurs."

You can practice these responses so that you are more likely to see the curveball. One of the last activities that I have presenters do before a big sales presentation is brainstorm any and all possible questions that the potential clients could throw at them. We then go through every question, one at a time, and come up with an example or story in response. By the time the team enters the question and answer period in the real presentation, every member will have already delivered a well-designed and flawlessly delivered speech to the committee and will have edified one another and presented as a solid team. And the team will already be prepared for anything that could come up in a question and answer session, so they are loaded for bear when the first question is asked.

Remember that the main reason for delivering the interview presentation is to get the decision makers to like you. If you answer their challenging questions with stories, you will appear confident and in control. They will often ask only a couple of challenging questions if you answer those first few questions well.

CHAPTER 10

Seven Deadly Sins That Will
Turn Off Audiences

"An error doesn't become a mistake until you refuse to correct it."
—Orlando A. Battista

In this book, we have covered (1) why you need to be a great presenter in order to be viewed as the expert, (2) how to design clear and concise persuasive presentations, (3) how to add impact to your presentations, (4) where to speak, and (5) how to generate additional revenue when you speak. In this chapter, we'll cover a few traps that presenters often fall into that can really turn off the audience. The reason why I have waited until the end of the book to cover these "sins" is that if you do the things that I've outlined in the earlier chapters, you will easily avoid each of these sins.

We'll start with the least offensive to audiences and work our way up to the absolute biggest mistake that presenters can make.

SIN #1: GOING OVER TIME WITHOUT PERMISSION

Going over the allotted time can cause a number of challenges for both you and any other speakers, and for every minute that you go over, you can subtract an equal amount of morale and enthusiasm for your topic. The way that most presenters prepare for their speeches actually causes this challenge. Most presenters have either memorized a speech or will prepare a bullet point for every idea that they intend to cover. As they deliver their presentations, if they elaborate on any specific point, they will have to make up the time difference somewhere else in the presentation. Often, presenters in these situations compensate by either skipping points or breezing through the latter part of the presentation. If the presenter gets too far off track, it can be impossible to make up the time.

However, presenters who cover only a few key concepts and use solid evidence such as stories, examples, and analogies to explain each point as we've discussed in this book can hit an allotted time period almost exactly. If the presenter finds that the presentation is running short, he or she can elaborate a little and give more details in the stories or examples being used. If the presenter is running long, more abbreviated versions of the stories can be given, and some of the evidence can be cut altogether. For instance, if you have five key points in your entire presentation and you prepare three solid pieces of evidence for each of the five points, you have the ability to use only two of the three pieces of evidence that you prepared for your latter points if you start to run long.

Speakers who are able to hit an exact time period without delivering a "stump speech" (one that you have practiced over and over and over to hit an exact time) are extremely rare. That is why when you attend conventions and banquets with a number of different speakers during the day, those who speak late in the day are almost always off their outlined agenda (usually running long). When you practice and master the presentation structure that we outlined in this book, and you learn to hit your time frame *exactly,* you will instantly move into an elite class of highly sought after presenters. You also gain an incredible amount of respect from your audience.

SIN #2: USING USELESS WORDS

Err, uhm, and *you know* are what we call word-whiskers, and when a speaker is nervous, these filler words can become somewhat annoying if they overshadow the actual presentation. These word-whiskers can hurt your chances of being seen as the expert, but only if the occurrence of these filler words is excessive.

For instance, a few years back after Barack Obama was elected president, Hillary Clinton became his secretary of state, and Caroline Kennedy (John F. Kennedy's daughter) threw her hat into the ring to fill Clinton's now-vacant Senate seat. She was the crowd favorite until she did her first national TV interview. In the first 3 minutes of her interview, she said, "Ya know" more than 40 times, and it just got worse from there. Shortly after the interview after experiencing days of ridicule, she removed her name from consideration entirely. So, yes, these word-whiskers can affect an audience's perception of you.

However, the more you focus on the filler words, the more you will actually use them. Whatever you focus on, you will get more of. So if you focus on *not* saying filler words, you will likely end up saying them more often. What's more, if you eliminate these words entirely, you will sound kind of odd. Many toasting clubs and adult presentation courses will have someone who counts *uhms* in the group, which is a huge mistake. The *uhms* are a symptom, so if you just try to mask the symptom, it's like seeing the check engine light on your car dashboard and deciding to eliminate the light by crawling under the dashboard and snipping the wire to turn it off. Sure, you don't see the light anymore, but the engine still needs repair. *Uhms* work the same way. You can train yourself to avoid the *uhms* if you spend a lot of time and effort, but it is a lot easier to just eliminate the cause.

The biggest cause of word-whiskers is bullet points. Specifically, this occurs when a presenter has 10 bullet points on one slide and each bullet point is just a couple of words that the presenter is using as a prompt to remember details about what he or she wants to talk about. Each time the presenter reads the next bullet point, he or she has to pause and remember what the heck it was that he or she wanted to say about that point. Nervousness shoots up, and the word-whiskers appear. "Uh, this bullet point was . . . uh . . . "

So what is the solution? Fewer bullet points supported by a story or example will always do the trick. Stories, especially personal experiences, are easy to deliver, because the presenter just plays the video in his or her head and describes what happened. Since this delivery is so much easier, the nervousness drops dramatically, and so does the number of *errs* and *uhms*.

SIN #3—SPEAKING IN A MONOTONE VOICE

Presenters without emotion are often described as being monotone or boring. Again, this is a symptom of a poorly designed presentation. If the presenter has all of his or her ideas on a PowerPoint slide and the delivery is in a read . . . click . . . read . . . click style, then it is much more difficult to add energy or enthusiasm to the presentation.

Next time you are at a bar or a party, look around the room and watch what everyone is doing. You will likely see people grouped together around tables. The energy around the tables will often be fairly high because the people around these tables will be building rapport with one another by sharing stories. Sometimes the stories will be funny. Sometimes the stories will be shocking. Sometimes the stories will be sad. But the stories will almost always have some emotion attached to them. As you look around the bar or party, you will probably not describe any of the speakers as boring, and none of them will likely have a monotone delivery. Interestingly, no one ever brings a slide show or projector to the bar for help, and no one ever has to rely on notes.

When you are communicating with your audience, use the techniques that work with your friends and add in stories or some of the other impact ideas that I covered earlier in the book. This will make the monotone voice go away.

SIN #4—SPEAKING SHOPTALK

Shoptalk is semantics related to a specific industry. If you have ever watched a television hospital drama, you'll hear a lot of shoptalk, like *EKG, MRI, angioplasty, ABG, CBC, stent,* and many more. Accountants use terms such as *accrual method, double entry, net income, IBIT,* and *balance sheet.* Engineers have really cool terms such as *apron, backwater, bedding, CMP, cutoff wall,* and *directional drilling.* Even restaurants have terminology; in fact, companies like The Waffle House

poke fun at restaurant terminology by having customers order their hash browns using semantics like *smothered and covered* (my favorite), but other restaurants have terms like *bev nap, Cambro, dupe, in the weeds,* and even *stretch it.* The point is that every industry has its slang or acronyms, but these terms can be very confusing to new people, to audience members outside of the industry, and, often, to the very people who the presenter would expect to know the terms.

Even if the people in your audience know the terms, they will still often have to pause, think about the terms, and then jump back into the presentation. This means, for just a second, you will lose your audience if you use shoptalk during your presentation. A little will be overlooked, but if you rely heavily on confusing terms to explain your points, you will likely turn off the audience.

So why do people do it? Why do presenters load up their presentations with complicated terms? Most often, if presenters think that the audience will be judging their intelligence (whether the audience actually is or not), the presenters will try to make themselves sound smarter by using what they think are intelligent terms in the presentation. A lot of new speakers will fall into this trap. Also speakers who present to audiences who have education credentials will fall into this trap. Presenters in these cases will often think, "I can't let the audience figure out just how much smarter they all are than I am," and will compensate with intelligent-sounding shoptalk.

If you find yourself falling into this trap, try to think about the entire presentation process differently. If people are taking time out of their busy day to listen to you, it is because you have information that they either want or need. For the topic that you are presenting on, you are the expert, not the audience. You have the cookie. So you don't need to impress the audience with your "Harvard words." You'll have much better success if you use your content and delivery style, instead of industry semantics, to impress the audience.

By the way, not to keep harping on stories and examples, but even if you use shoptalk, if you use a real-life story to explain your point, your audience will still understand you perfectly. (Are you starting to realize just why stories and examples are so important to the success of a presentation?)

SIN #5—SPEAKING WHILE THE AUDIENCE IS READING YOUR SLIDE

Overly complicated or busy slides cause this challenge. If you have too much information on a slide, or if your slide shows a complicated chart or graph, your audience will stop focusing on what you are saying the moment you show the slide. The easy solution is to insert only visual aids into your presentation that add clarity and help you better explain the point you are making. If you have charts or graphs, rather than putting them on slides, it's often better to create a handout for your audience or an oversized board as a visual aid.

When one of our Fearless Presentations instructors teaches a two-day class, that instructor will use no more than 20 slides for the entire two-day presentation. Participants in the class learn how to give entire presentations using only one concise slide as a visual aid. When I teach a two-day Entrepreneur Boot Camp, I will often use only about 25 slides total, and a number of those slides are used for funny videos that we show during breaks. Remember that the PowerPoint slide show is not your presentation. It should be a visual aid for your presentation.

SIN #6—READING THE ENTIRE SLIDE OR VISUAL AID TO THE AUDIENCE

The more PowerPoint focused your presentation is, the less your audience will see you as the expert. Remember that your experience related to the topic is your key to people seeing you as a go-to person in the industry. So if you just quote statistics from a PowerPoint slide, the audience will think, "Why didn't the speaker just send us the slide show? I can read the slides myself." Again, if you design your slide show well, this problem will go away automatically.

SIN #7—DUMPING DATA ON THE AUDIENCE

The absolute biggest complaint that audiences make about presenters is that the presenter gave too much information in too short a period of time. Remember that the audience is going to remember or retain only three to five key points; so if you give 10 points, 20 points, 30 points, or 150 points in one sitting, you will lose the audience almost immediately. The biggest thing to keep in mind about data dumping is that it doesn't matter how funny you are, how entertaining

you are, how interesting you are, or how interactive you are; if you give your audience too much data or too much information, you will lose them somewhere along the way.

Most people aren't aware that the keynote speaker at the ceremony where President Lincoln delivered the Gettysburg Address was Edward Everett, a well-known and renowned speaker of his time. He spoke for 2 hours and delivered inspirational rhetoric that engaged the crowd. Shortly after Everett finished his keynote speech, Lincoln stood up and delivered the Gettysburg Address, which took just under 2 minutes and is probably the most quoted speech in American history. Everett took to the stage one more time as Lincoln sat back down, and legend has it that he turned to Lincoln and said, "Mr. President, you said more in 2 minutes than I did in 2 hours."

If you are a great presenter and you give your audience more than a few key points, then your audience may remember some of your content. But you as the presenter don't have any control over which of your key points the audience remembers. By being concise and using the concepts I outlined in this book, you will be a much more successful presenter.

MASTER YOUR PRESENTATIONS AND AVOID THESE DEADLY SINS

If you want to master your presentations, just follow these presentation secrets, and you can't lose.

- Start by identifying what your audience wants and needs.
- Create a title (topic) that states a result that your audience wants.
- Limit your presentation to three to five key points.

- Add stories, analogies, and other impact ideas to prove each of your key points.
- Now design your slide show as a way to add clarity.

If you follow these simple presentation secrets, you will eliminate each of the seven deadly sins of presentations and will move into an elite segment of presenters who can inform, persuade, and entertain their audiences every single time.

What's Next?

When you read a book, you gain information, but the information or knowledge is worthless until you actually put it into practice. When you apply the principles in this book, if you have what you perceive to be a success, your confidence will skyrocket. However, if you have what you perceive to be a failure, your confidence will shrink and your fear of public speaking will grow. Public speaking is a difficult skill to master on your own, so a good coach is well worth the small investment. If you feel at all nervous or apprehensive about using these skills out in the real world, then I'd like to invite you to attend one of our classes or coaching sessions.

- **Fearless Presentations:** The Fearless Presentations class is a two-day coaching seminar offered in every major city in the United States and Canada as well as in a number of cities in Europe. The first half of the class focuses on helping participants eliminate their fear of public speaking, and the latter half helps participants design and deliver impactful and persuasive presentations from scratch in just minutes. Since 2001, more than 12,000 people have attended this class, and we've never had even a single person fail to reduce his or her nervousness exponentially. For a schedule of upcoming classes or to register for a course, visit the Fearless Presentations website at www .FearlessPresentations.com.

- **Entrepreneur Boot Camp:** The Leader's Institute Entrepreneur Boot Camp is a workshop designed to help small-business owners overcome some of the most challenging parts of being a small-business owner. In addition to helping entrepreneurs use presentation skills to become recognized experts in their industries, the sessions also cover leadership skills that improve communication, reduce conflict, and build the next generation of leaders for their businesses. Business owners know that it is a lot easier to add new clients and customers to a business when prospects call the business instead of the business having to call on prospective customers, so the Boot Camp outlines specific marketing skills that create an endless supply of potential new customers as well. Most entrepreneurs hit a ceiling at some point in their existence. The first barrier occurs at about the $300,000 mark in gross revenue. The second occurs at about the $1 million mark. The third occurs at the $10 million mark. If you are a business owner who has hit any of these revenue ceilings and you want to crash through that ceiling this year, then the Entrepreneur Boot Camp is for you. Classes are forming in select cities throughout the United States. For information or to register for a class, visit the Boot Camp website at www .LeadersInstituteBootCamp.com.

- **Keynote Speeches:** Doug Staneart is a dynamic keynote speaker, specializing in presentation skills as well as topics related to developing leadership and building a team culture. In 2005, Doug revolutionized the team-building industry when he created the Build-a-Bike team-building workshop that combined high-energy team activities with philanthropic donations to local charities and he created a brand-new industry. His most popular topics are *Creating a Team Culture, Cultivating Customers, Fearless Presentations,* and *Presentation Secrets.* Doug is based in Dallas/Fort Worth, but he has delivered keynote speeches in cities all over the world. To schedule Doug for a keynote speech or to check his availability, visit www.DougStaneart.com.